HACKING

with

KALI LINUX

Julian Snow

HACKING WITH KALI LINUX

the information herein, either directly or indirectly.

Respective authors own all copyrights not held by the publisher.

The information herein is offered for informational purposes solely, and is universal as so. The presentation of the information is without contract or any type of guarantee assurance.

The trademarks that are used are without any consent, and the publication of the trademark is without permission or backing by the trademark owner. All trademarks and brands within this book are for clarifying purposes only and are the owned by the owners themselves, not affiliated with this document.

Disclaimer

All erudition contained in this book is given for informational and educational purposes only. The author is not in any way accountable for any results or outcomes that emanate from using this material. Constructive attempts have been made to provide information that is both accurate and effective, but the author is not bound for the accuracy or use/misuse of this information.

Table of Contents

INTRODUCTION

Hackers are currently utilizing increasingly modern methods to focus on the frameworks. People, little scale organizations or enormous association, are for the most part being affected. In this way, every one of these organizations whether IT or non-IT firms have comprehended the significance of Cyber Security and concentrating on receiving every conceivable measure to manage digital dangers.

With the game up for digital dangers and programmers, associations and their workers should make a stride head to manage them. As we like to associate everything to the web, this additionally builds the odds of vulnerabilities, breaks, and imperfections.

Gone are the days when passwords were sufficient to secure the framework and its information. We as a whole need to secure our own and expert information, and in this way Cyber Security is the thing that you should know to guarantee information assurance.

Thus, lets being with characterizing the term Cyber Security.

Digital Security is the procedure and methods engaged with ensuring touchy information, PC frameworks, systems and programming applications from digital assaults. The digital assaults are general phrasing which covers countless points, however a portion of the prominent are:

Altering frameworks and information put away inside

Misuse of assets

Unapproved access to the focused on framework and getting to touchy data

Upsetting typical working of the business and its procedures

Utilizing ransomware assaults to encode information and coerce cash from unfortunate casualties

The assaults are presently winding up progressively inventive and complex that is fit for disturbing the security and hacking the frameworks. So it's trying for each business and security expert to defeat this test and battle back with these assaults.

To comprehend the requirement for Cyber Security measures and its practices, how about we have a fast take a gander at the sorts of dangers and assaults.

CHAPTER ONE

The basics of cyber security

Ransomware is a document encryption programming program that uses an extraordinary strong encryption calculation to scramble the records on the objective framework.

The creators of the Ransomware risk produce a remarkable decoding key for every one of its unfortunate casualties and spare it in a remote server. In this manner, clients can't get to their records by any application.

The ransomware creators exploit this and request an impressive payoff sum from the unfortunate casualties to give the decoding code or unscramble the information. In any case, such assaults have any assurance of recuperation of information even subsequent to paying the payment.

Botnets Attacks

Botnets was at first intended to complete a particular undertakings inside a gathering.

It is characterized as a system or gathering of gadgets associated with a similar system to execute an errand. In any case, this is currently being utilized by awful entertainers and programmers that endeavors to get to the system and infuse any noxious code or malware to disturb its working. A portion of the botnet assaults include:

Appropriated Denial of Service (DDoS) assaults

Spreading spam messages

Taking of secret information

Botnets assaults are for the most part completed against enormous scale organizations and association because of its immense information get to. Through this assault, the programmers can control countless gadgets and bargain them for its abhorrent thought processes.

Social building are presently a typical strategies utilized by digital culprits to assemble client's touchy data.

It might deceive you by showing alluring commercials, prizes, colossal offers thus and request that you feed your own and financial balance subtleties. All the data you enter there is cloned and utilized for monetary fakes, character fakes thus.

It merits saying about the ZEUS infection that is dynamic since 2007 and is being utilized as a social building assault techniques to take banking subtleties of the people in question. Alongside money related misfortunes, Social designing assaults are fit for downloading other damaging dangers to the concerned framework.

Digital currency seizing is the new expansion to this digital world.

As the advanced money and mining are getting to be prominent, so it is among digital culprits. They have discovered their abhorrent advantage to the cryptographic money mining which includes complex registering to mine virtual cash like Bitcoin, Ethereum, Monero, Litecoin so on.

Digital money financial specialists and brokers are the vulnerable objective for this assault.

Digital money capturing otherwise called "Cryptojacking". It is a program intended to infuse mining codes quietly to the framework. In this way the programmer quietly utilizes the CPU, GPU and power assets of the assaulted framework to dig for the digital currency.

The system is utilized to especially mine Monero coins. As the mining is an unpredictable procedure, it devours the greater part of the CPU assets which effects the framework's presentation. Additionally, it is done under the entirety of your costs, so the unfortunate casualty may get ha gigantic power bill and web bill.

It likewise decreases the life expectancy of the influenced gadget.

Phishing is a deceitful activity of sending spam messages by copying to be from any real source.

Such sends have a solid title with connections like a receipt, employment propositions, enormous ideas from legitimate delivery administrations or any significant mail from higher authorities of the organization.

The phishing trick assaults are the most widely recognized digital assaults that plans to take delicate information. Like Login qualifications, Visa numbers, financial balance data, etc. To maintain a strategic distance from this, you ought to become familiar with phishing email crusades and its preventive measures. One can likewise utilize email sifting innovations to keep away from this assault.

Alongside these, 2019 will look for the potential in biometric assaults, AI assaults and IoT assaults. Numerous organizations and associations are seeing enormous scale digital assaults and there is no stop for them. In spite of the steady security investigation and updates, the ascent of digital risk is predictable. In this way, it is worth to teach yourself with the fundamentals of cybersecurity and its usage.

The Cyber Security on an entire is an exceptionally wide term however depends on three crucial ideas known as "The CIA Triad".

It comprises of Confidentiality, Integrity and Availability. This model is intended to manage the association with the arrangements of Cyber Security in the domain of Information security.

It characterizes the principles that restrains the penetrationof data. Classification takes on the measures to limit the delicate data from being gotten to by digital aggressors and programmers.

In an association, people groups are permitted or precluded the penetrationfrom claiming data as indicated by its class by approving the correct people in a division. They are additionally given appropriate preparing about the sharing of data and protecting their records with solid passwords.

They can change the manner in which information is taken care of inside an association to guarantee information security. Different approaches to guarantee secrecy, similar to: two-factor confirmation, Data encryption, information characterization, biometric check, and security tokens.

This guarantees the information is predictable, precise and reliable over its timeframe. It implies that the information inside the travel ought not be changed, adjusted, erased or illicitly being gotten to. Appropriate measures ought to be taken in an association to guarantee its wellbeing. Document consents and client access control are the measures controlling the information rupture. Likewise, there ought to be apparatuses and innovations actualized to recognize any change or break in the information. Different Organizations utilizes a checksum, and even cryptographic checksum to confirm the trustworthiness of information.

To adapt to information misfortune or inadvertent erasure or even digital assaults, customary reinforcements ought to be there. Cloud reinforcements are presently the most confided in answer for this.

Accessibility as far as every fundamental part like equipment, programming, systems, gadgets and security gear should all be kept up and redesigned. This will guarantee the smooth working and access of Data with no interruption. Likewise giving steady correspondence between the segments through giving enough data transfer capacity.

It additionally includes choosing additional security hardware if there should arise an occurrence of any calamity or bottlenecks. Utilities like firewalls, catastrophe recuperation plans, intermediary servers and a legitimate reinforcement arrangement ought to guarantee to adapt to DoS assaults.

For an effective methodology, it ought to experience numerous layers of security to guarantee insurance to each constituent of CyberSecurity. Especially including PCs, equipment frameworks, systems, programming programs and the information which are shared among them.

In an association, to achieve a powerful Cyber Security approach, the people groups, forms, PCs, systems and innovation of an association either enormous or little ought to be similarly capable. In the event that all part will supplement one another, at that point, it is especially conceivable to remain against the intense digital danger and assaults.

PCs and the Internet have turned out to be fundamental for homes and associations alike. The reliance on them increments constantly, be it for family unit clients, in mission basic space control, control framework the executives, therapeutic applications or for corporate money frameworks. Yet additionally in parallel are the provokes identified with the proceeded and solid conveyance of administration which is turning into a greater worry for associations. Digital security is at the cutting edge of all dangers that the associations face, with a lion's share rating it higher than the risk of fear mongering or a cataclysmic event.

Despite all the center Cyber security has had, it has been a difficult voyage up until now. The worldwide spend on IT Security is required to hit $120 Billion by 2017 [4], and that is one region where the IT spending plan for most organizations either remained level or somewhat expanded even in the ongoing money related emergencies [5]. However, that has not significantly decreased the quantity of vulnerabilities in programming or assaults by criminal gatherings.

The US Government has been getting ready for a "Digital Pearl Harbor" [18] style hard and fast assault that may deaden basic administrations, and even reason physical decimation of property and lives. It is required to be organized from the criminal underbelly of nations like China, Russia or North Korea.

There is a need to on a very basic level reconsider our way to deal with verifying our IT frameworks. Our way to deal with security is siloed and spotlights on point arrangements so far for explicit dangers like enemy of infections, spam channels, interruption identifications and firewalls [6]. Be that as it may, we are at a phase where Cyber frameworks are significantly more than simply tin-and-wire and programming. They include fundamental issues with a social, financial and political segment. The interconnectedness of frameworks, entwined with a people component makes IT frameworks un-isolable from the human component. Complex Cyber frameworks today nearly have their very own existence; Cyber frameworks are intricate versatile frameworks that we have attempted to comprehend and handle utilizing increasingly conventional hypotheses.

Before getting into the inspirations of regarding a Cyber framework as a Complex framework, here is a brief of what a Complex framework is. Note that the expression "framework" could be any blend of individuals, procedure or innovation that satisfies a specific reason. The wrist watch you are wearing, the sub-maritime reefs, or the economy of a nation - are for the most part instances of a "framework".

In exceptionally basic terms, a Complex framework is any framework wherein the pieces of the framework and their associations together speak to a particular conduct, with the end goal that an investigation of all its constituent parts can't clarify the conduct. In such frameworks the circumstances and logical results can not really be connected and the connections are non-straight - a little change could have an unbalanced effect. As such, as Aristotle said "the entire is more prominent than the aggregate of its parts". One of the most prominent models utilized in this setting is of a urban traffic framework and development of car influxes; examination of individual vehicles and vehicle drivers can't help clarify the examples and rise of roads turned parking lots.

While a Complex Adaptive framework (CAS) likewise has qualities of self-learning, rise and development among the members of the mind boggling framework. The members or specialists in a CAS show heterogeneous conduct. Their conduct and connections with different specialists consistently developing. The key qualities for a framework to be portrayed as Complex Adaptive may be:

Oneself learning procedure of specialists depends on "Transformations" and "Hybrids" - two essential administrators in Genetic Algorithm usage. They imitate the DNA hybrid and changes in natural development of living things. Through hybrids and changes, specialists gain from their own encounters and errors. These could be utilized to reenact the learning conduct of potential aggressors, without the need to physically envision all the utilization cases and client travels that an assailant may attempt to break a Cyber framework with.

Multifaceted nature in Cyber frameworks, particularly the utilization of Agent Based displaying to evaluate the rising conduct of frameworks is a moderately new field of concentrate with next to no exploration done on it yet. There is still some best approach before utilizing Agent Based Modeling turns into a business recommendation for associations. In any case, given the emphasis on Cyber security and insufficiencies in our present position, Complexity science is absolutely a road that professionals and the scholarly community are expanding their attention on.

The term 'Programmer' was begat during the

1960s at the Massachusetts Institute of Technology to portray specialists who utilized their abilities to re-create centralized server frameworks, expanding their proficiency and enabling them to perform various tasks.

These days, the term routinely portrays talented developers who addition unapproved access into PC frameworks by misusing shortcomings or utilizing bugs, spurred either by vindictiveness or fiendishness. For instance, a programmer can make calculations to break passwords, enter organizes, or even upset system administrations.

With the expanded ubiquity of the Internet and E-Commerce, malevolent hacking turned into the most generally known structure, an impression strengthened by its delineation in different types of news media and diversion. Guideline speaking, the essential thought process of vindictive/exploitative hacking includes taking profitable data or monetary benefit.

All things considered, not all hacking is terrible. This carries us to the second kind of hacking: Ethical hacking. Ethical programmers are procured by associations to investigate the vulnerabilities of their frameworks and arranges and create answers for forestall information ruptures. Think of it as a cutting-edge change of the familiar axiom "It takes a hoodlum to get a cheat."

CHAPTER TWO

The mean of ethical hacking and types

Ethical Hacking is an approved routine with regards to bypassing framework security to distinguish potential information ruptures and dangers in a system. The organization that claims the framework or system permits Cyber Security specialists to perform such exercises so as to test the framework's safeguards. In this manner, not at all like pernicious hacking, this procedure is arranged, affirmed, and all the more significantly, legitimate.

Ethical programmers plan to examine the framework or system for powerless focuses that pernicious programmers can abuse or decimate. They gather and break down the data to make sense of approaches to fortify the security of the framework/organize/applications. Thusly, they can improve the security impression so it can all the more likely withstand assaults or redirect them.

The act of Ethical hacking is designated "White Hat" hacking, and the individuals who perform it are called White Hat programmers. As opposed to Ethical Hacking, "Dark Hat" hacking portrays works on including security infringement. The Black Hat programmers utilize unlawful procedures to bargain the framework or obliterate data.

Not at all like White Hat programmers, "Dim Hat" programmers don't request authorization before getting into your framework. Be that as it may, Gray Hats are additionally not quite the same as Black Hats since they don't perform hacking for any close to home or outsider advantage. These programmers don't have any malevolent expectation and hack frameworks for entertainment only or different reasons, more often than not advising the proprietor about any dangers they find. Dark Hat and Black Hat hacking are both unlawful as the two of them establish an unapproved framework break, despite the fact that the goals of the two sorts of programmers vary.

The most ideal approach to separate between White Hat and Black Hat programmers is by investigating their intentions. Dark Hat programmers are inspired by malevolent goal, showed by of individual increases, benefit, or provocation; though White Hat programmers search out and cure vulnerabilities, in order to keep Black Hats from exploiting.

Different approaches to draw a differentiation between White Hat and Black Hat programmers include:

Procedures utilized: White Hat programmers copy the strategies and techniques pursued by malevolent programmers so as to discover the framework inconsistencies, recreating all the last's means to discover how a framework assault happened or may happen. On the off chance that they locate a powerless point in the framework or system, they report it quickly and fix the imperfection.

Lawfulness: Even however White Hat hacking pursues indistinguishable procedures and strategies from Black Hat hacking, just one is legitimately worthy. Dark Hat programmers violate the law by entering frameworks without assent.

Possession: White Hat programmers are utilized by associations to enter their frameworks and identify security issues. Dark cap programmers neither possess the framework nor work for somebody who claims it.

Jobs and Responsibilities of an Ethical Hacker

Ethical Hackers must pursue certain rules so as to perform hacking legitimately. A decent programmer knows their obligation and clings to the majority of the Ethical rules. Here are the most significant principles of Ethical Hacking:

A Ethical programmer must look for approval from the association that possesses the framework. Programmers ought to acquire total endorsement before playing out any security appraisal on the framework or system.

Decide the extent of their evaluation and make known their arrangement to the association.

Report any security breaks and vulnerabilities found in the framework or system.

Keep their revelations secret. As their motivation

is to verify the framework or system, Ethical programmers ought to consent to and regard their non-divulgence understanding.

Eradicate all hints of the hack in the wake of checking the framework for any defenselessness. It keeps malignant programmers from entering the framework through the distinguished provisos.

Ethical Hacking is a difficult territory of concentrate as it requires dominance of everything that makes up a framework or system. This is the reason affirmations have turned out to be well known among yearning Ethical programmers.

With applicable Ethical Hacking confirmations, you can propel your vocation in cybersecurity in the accompanying ways:

Confirmed people realize how to configuration, fabricate, and keep up a safe business condition. In the event that you can exhibit your insight in these zones, you will be precious with regards to examining dangers and formulating successful arrangements.

Ensured cybersecurity experts have better pay prospects contrasted with their non-confirmed friends. As per Payscale, Certified Ethical Hackers procure a normal compensation of $90K in the U.S.

Confirmation approves your aptitudes in the field of IT security and makes you progressively detectable while applying for testing work jobs.

With the developing occurrences of security breaks, associations are putting gigantically in IT security and lean toward affirmed contender for their association.

New companies need profoundly talented experts experienced in repulsing digital dangers. A confirmation can enable you to show your IT security abilities to acquire lucrative occupations at new businesses.

In this day and age, cybersecurity has turned into a drifting subject of expanding enthusiasm among numerous organizations. With noxious programmers discovering more current approaches to break the barriers of systems consistently, the job of Ethical programmers has turned out to be progressively significant over all parts. It has made a plenty of chances for cybersecurity experts and has motivated people to take up Ethical hacking as their profession. Along these lines, on the off chance that you have ever thought about the potential outcomes of getting into the cybersecurity space, or even simply upskilling, this is the ideal time to do as such. What's more, obviously the most proficient method for achieving this is by getting guaranteed in Ethical hacking, and the most ideal approach to do that is to let Simplilearn help you accomplish it! Look at them now, and join the battle for secure frameworks

In the beginning of worldwide clashes, psychological oppressor associations financing cybercriminals to break security frameworks, either to bargain national security highlights or to blackmail tremendous sums by infusing malware and denying access. Bringing about the relentless ascent of cybercrime. Associations face the test of refreshing hack-averting strategies, introducing a few advancements to secure the framework before succumbing to the programmer.

New worms, malware, infections, and ransomware are increasing each day and is making a requirement for Ethical hacking administrations to shield the systems of organizations, government offices or barrier.

Programmers are of various kinds and are named dependent on their purpose of the hacking framework. Extensively, there are two primary programmers – White-Hat programmer and Black-Hat programmer. The names are gotten from old Spaghetti Westerns, where the hero wears a white cap and the trouble maker wears a dark cap.

The Certified Ethical Hacker (C|EH) credentialing and preparing system given by EC-Council is a regarded and believed Ethical hacking program in the business. Since the beginning of Certified Ethical Hacker in 2003, the qualification has turned out to be perhaps the best alternative for businesses and organizations over the world. The C|EH test is ANSI 17024 consistent, adding worth and validity to qualification individuals. It is likewise recorded as a pattern accreditation in the US Department of Defense (DoD) Directive 8570 and is a GCT (GCHQ Certified Training).

Today, you can discover Certified Ethical Hackers working with probably the best and biggest organizations crosswise over enterprises like medicinal services, money related, government, vitality and significantly more!

A Ethical programmer, additionally alluded to as a white cap programmer, is a data security master who deliberately endeavors to enter a PC framework, system, application or other registering asset in the interest of its proprietors - and with their authorization - to discover security vulnerability

What are the type of hackers and what is the Ethical Hacking

There are a number of ways ethical hackers can help organizations, including:

Finding vulnerabilities. Ethical hackers help companies determine which of their IT security measures are effective, which need to be updated and which contain vulnerabilities that can be exploited. When ethical hackers finish evaluating organizations' systems, they report back to company leaders about those vulnerable areas, for instance, a lack of sufficient password encryption, insecure applications or exposed systems running unpatched software. Organizations can use the data from these tests to make informed decisions about where and how to improve their security posture to prevent cyberattacks.

Demonstrating methods used by cybercriminals. These demonstrations show executives the hacking techniques that malicious actors use to attack their systems and wreak havoc with their businesses. Companies that have in-depth knowledge of the methods the attackers use to break into their systems are better able to prevent them from doing so.

Helping prepare for a cyberattack. Cyberattacks can cripple or destroy a business, especially a small business. However, most companies are completely unprepared for cyberattacks. Ethical hackers understand how threat actors operate and they know how these bad actors will use new information and techniques to attack systems. Security professionals who work with ethical hackers are better able to prepare for future attacks because they can better react to the constantly changing nature of online threats.

Ethical hacking techniques

Ethical hackers generally use the same hacking skills that malicious actors use to attack enterprises. Some of these hacking techniques include:

Scanning ports to find vulnerabilities. Ethical hackers use port scanning tools, such as Nmap, Nessus or Wireshark, to scan a company's systems, identify open ports, study the vulnerabilities of each port and take remedial action.

Scrutinizing patch installation processes to be sure that they don't introduce new vulnerabilities in the updated software that can be exploited.

Performing network traffic analysis and sniffing by using appropriate tools.

Attempting to evade intrusion detection systems, intrusion prevention systems, honeypots and firewalls.

Ethical hackers also rely on social engineering techniques to manipulate end users and obtain information about an organization's computing environment. Like black hat hackers, ethical hackers rummage through postings on social media or GitHub, engage employees in phishing attacks through email or roam through premises with a clipboard to exploit vulnerabilities in physical security. However, there are social engineering techniques that ethical hackers should not use, such as making physical threats to employees or other types of attempt to extort access or information.

How to become an ethical hacker

There are no standard education criteria for an ethical hacker, so an organization can set its own requirements for that position. Those interested in pursuing a career as an ethical hacker should consider a bachelor's or master's degree in information security, computer science or even mathematics as a strong foundation.

Individuals not planning to attend college can consider pursing an information security career in the military. Many organizations consider a military background a plus for information security hiring, and some organizations are required to hire individuals with security clearances.

Other technical subjects including programming, scripting, networking and hardware engineering, can help those pursuing a career as ethical hackers by offering a fundamental understanding of the underlying technologies that form the systems that they will be working on. Other pertinent technical skills include system administration and software development.

Certified ethical hackers

There are a number of ethical hacking

certifications as well as IT certifications related to security that can help individuals become ethical hackers, including:

Certified Ethical Hacker (CEH): This is a vendor-neutral certification from the EC-Council, one of the leading certification bodies. This security certification, which validates how much an individual knows about network security, is best suited for a penetration tester role. This certification covers more than 270 attacks technologies. Prerequisites for this certification include attending official training offered by the EC-Council or its affiliates and having at least two years of information security-related experience.

Certified Information Systems Auditor (CISA): This certification is offered by ISACA, a nonprofit, independent association that advocates for professionals involved in information security, assurance, risk management and governance. The exam certifies the knowledge and skills of security professionals. To qualify for this certification, candidates must have five years of professional work experience related to information systems auditing, control or security.

Certified information security manager (CISM): CISM is an advanced certification offered by ISACA that provides validation for individuals who have demonstrated the in-depth knowledge and experience required to develop and manage an enterprise information security program. The certification is aimed at information security managers, aspiring managers or IT consultants who support information security program management.

GIAC Security Essentials (GSEC): This certification created and administered by the Global Information Assurance Certification organization is geared toward security professionals who want to demonstrate they are qualified for IT systems hands-on roles with respect to security tasks. Candidates are required to demonstrate they understand information security beyond simple terminology and concepts.

When people first hear about hacking, they will

usually see this idea as something negative. Indeed, hacking has always been about taking advantage of unprotected or weakly-guarded sites or systems for the individuals own selfish interest. Because of this, others (often companies,) who want to strengthen the protection of their online systems turn to professionals for help. These professional hackers (sometimes known as "white hats,") use an ethical hacking methodology to help build a stronger defense against real hacking threats. By deliberately "attacking" the system, they can quickly identify its flaws, and then begin to come up with contingency plans to stall, avoid or eliminate real actual hacking attacks.

From the ethical hacking methodology, you can see that not all hacks are bad. The act of hacking ethically into a system in order to expose possible weak points, ones that real hackers, or "black hats" (due to less savoury intentions) can exploit, can help prevent the company from loss of earnings or reputation. Indeed, a lot of companies are now seeking the services of those who can perform this task because they understand that the only way to fight against skilled hackers is with another skilled hacker of their own!

Those with a strong understanding of computer systems can train to carry out these services. Though when you consider the ethical hacking methodology includes breaking into online systems, it is quite possible that many white hats today have gained their experiences originally as black hats themselves!

So long as your actions have been permitted by the company who owns the system, the mischief or disorder that you'll create during the hacking process will entirely benefit the company so long as they follow up and eliminate those weaknesses.

Ethical hackers are either hired professionals who have made a name for themselves as black hat hackers, or are real employees of the company who are knowledgeable enough to perform the task.

This is not about good or bad hackers, white hats or black hats; ultimately it is about the benefit of the company, and the protection of sensitive data they may hold. If you had a less desirable past (black hat,) but have since decided to work for the system than against it, you will be well cared for because of the service you can now provide.

The Ethical hacking procedure is tied in with getting results with regards to ensuring on the web frameworks against ruinous assaults. You are concerned uniquely with protecting the benefits and interests, and just by speculation and acting like a genuine programmer would this be able to be accomplished.

No ifs, ands or buts, this is a powerful method to shield from online dangers. In case you're an organization, don't falter to employ a white cap programmer, since they are outfitted with the correct learning and abilities to battle a danger from another programmer. Then again, in case you're engaged with hacking yourself, maybe there would be a profession for you to consider in chipping away at the opposite side?

While looking at hacking what do we will in general envision? An outlined figure in hoodie composing something in the PC, a dark screen, countless codes, a dull indoor, correct? In motion pictures, it just takes a couple of moments to rupture into a framework and get every one of the information. In any case, in actuality, it takes bunches of perspiration and blood to do the strategy called 'Hacking'.

It takes enormous diligent work, abilities, information, and energy to turn into an expert Ethical Hacker. Presently, the inquiry arrives, in what capacity can meddling into another person's database be Ethical? In spite of the fact that seems like an ironic expression, the facts demonstrate that the world needs white cap programmers now more than whenever previously. Business houses, law authorization cells, Government houses are needing gifted proficient Ethical programmers.

With the headway of innovation, similar to IT reappropriating, distributed computing, virtualization; we are presented to different security dangers consistently. All things considered, the systems administration specialists are contracted to shield database of a specific association from potential hurtful exploiters. Information misuse can prompt more prominent harm to notoriety and money related misfortune for any organization. Presently Ethical hacking is one of the most mainstream security practices performed on normal premise.

Digital wrongdoings have expanded greatly over the most recent couple of years. Ransomware like WannaCry, Petya is making news consistently with their different variations and it won't be a misrepresentation to state that they are digging in for the long haul expanding their muscle capacity to cause more mischief. Phishing plans, malware, digital undercover work, IP caricaturing and so forth are pervasive at this point. So as to defend information, organizations need to receive the proactive position.

With the consistently expanding prevalence of cloud comes things of security dangers. Presently, when business associations are utilizing cloud administrations like Google Drive, Microsoft Azure or Dropbox they are really putting away delicate information on an outsider device which might work to their greatest advantage. Utilizing outsider record sharing administrations really permits the information taken outside of the organization's IT condition. This frequently prompts a few security dangers including losing authority over delicate information, snooping, key administration, information spillage and so forth.

Pretty much all of us is dynamic on different long range informal communication destinations. We effectively share our whereabouts, interests, address, telephone numbers, date of birth there and with the data, it is simple for digital culprits to make sense of the injured individual's character or take their passwords. An investigation uncovers, around 60,000 Facebook profiles get bargained each day. Online networking clients are probably going to tap on unknown connections shared by companions or somebody they trust. This is an old technique for misusing unfortunate casualty's PC. Making counterfeit Facebook 'like' catches to pages is additionally a well known strategy for digital violations.

The meaning of system legal sciences and Ethical programmers has been advanced over the time. Numerous associations are yet to understand that the expense to ensure the organization database is significantly less than managing a grave digital assault to recuperate all information. Anticipation is in every case superior to fix. System legal sciences and Ethical programmers are contracted in IT parts to ceaselessly screen and distinguish potential vulnerabilities and make a move as indicated by that.

Associations must fuse progressed layered barrier, numerous danger location motors to recognize and lessen risk at the absolute first organize. Try not to fall into the snare of fancier risk strategies. The time has come to make genuine move to vanquish digital crooks in their own game.

The utilization of the expression "programmer" to signify a PC master with awful goals is a misnomer. A programmer is anybody with an abnormal state of PC aptitude, regardless of how the person utilizes it. Programmers come in three assortments: Black, white and dim. Dark, obviously, are pernicious; white are great programmers; and dim, as the name suggests, bounce between the two camps.

USA Today sees penetration("pen") analyzers, who additionally are called Ethical programmers. They progressively are being enlisted by organizations and security organizations to perceive what is working and what isn't. The piece gives a decent roundup. The most intriguing entry with regards to the piece includes the overall accomplishment of hacking from inside and outside the customer's office. The master says he is effective for all intents and purposes 100 percent of the time in accessing 80 percent to 90 percent of an organization's inner frameworks from inside. Alternately, solid edge resistances decrease his prosperity rate to 20 percent to 30 percent in the event that he begins from the opposite side of the firewall. In the case of nothing else, this demonstrates consideration regarding edge barrier in the course of recent years has been fruitful.

The potential advantages and noteworthy issues of infiltration testing are both on full see in an ongoing SC Magazine book, which reports on National Institute of Standards and Technology (NIST) suggestions that such systems be a normal device of government offices. The favorable circumstances are self-evident: Pen testing can help find and fix vulnerabilities before hoodlums or fear based oppressors do.

The drawback is that preparation individuals to do this is much the same as weapons preparing: There is no assurance the learning won't be turned on its source. Without a doubt, a significant part of the book portrays the oversight that must be practiced over such activities and the individuals who perform them. NIST prescribes that pariahs be utilized to ensure that individuals who work for an office don't make light of issues and to lessen the dangers of disappointed ex-representatives mounting an assault. The proposals will be concluded toward the part of the arrangement and distributed in March, the story says.

Unmistakably, this is an intriguing and hot field. It appears that pen testing quality shifts, and that the field is probably going to see much challenge. This is a decent review of Ethical hacking at Free Information Technology Tips. To begin with, the essayist portrays the agreement, which is known as an "escape correctional facility free" card since it discharges the programmer from criminal obligation. This is important on the grounds that quite a bit of what a Ethical programmer does is felonious. It is significant that an association counsel lawyers before drawing in a Ethical programmer. One evident issue: If an organization repays a programmer against arraignment, would the association still be subject if a customer brings a suit if the programmer commits an error and information is lost?

The piece depicts three things the individual attempts to discover: what data a programmer can get their hands on, what should be possible with that data and whether the association naturally would know whether a "genuine" programmer propelled an assault.

An ongoing take a gander at Ethical hacking all

in all and one specialist, David Jacquet, at Mainebiz follows the ascent of Ethical hacking and capably clarifies why these people are sought after. The annoying inquiry concerns the divisions between white, dark and dark. The universe of hacking is so specific and arcane, by what method would organizations be able to know for sure that the programmer they are welcoming to assault their systems genuinely is Ethical? How do associations realize that every one of the vulnerabilities found were accounted for to the client?

Apparently, it's a matter of notoriety and trust. Simultaneously, it's a somewhat troublesome supposition to make.

Does the word hacking alarm you? Incidentally it is hacking yet lawful hacking that is benefiting us. In the event that this is your first book on hacking, at that point clearly you will get some potential knowledge on hacking in the wake of perusing this. My book gives a basic outline on

Ethical programmers.

The term Ethical programmer came into surface in the late 1970s when the legislature of United States of America enlisted gatherings of specialists called 'red groups' to hack its own equipment and programming framework. Programmers are digital hoodlums or online PC offenders that training illicit hacking. They infiltrate into the security arrangement of a PC system to bring or concentrate data.

Innovation and web encouraged the birth and development of system disasters like infection, hostile to infection, hacking and Ethical hacking. Hacking is a routine with regards to alteration of a PC equipment and programming framework. Illicit breaking of a PC framework is a criminal offense. As of late a spurt in hacking of PC frameworks has opened up a few seminars on Ethical hacking.

A 'white cap' programmer is an ethical programmer who runs infiltration testing and interruption testing. Ethical hacking is legitimately hacking a PC framework and infiltrating into its database. It plans to verify the escape clauses and breaks in the digital security arrangement of an organization. Legitimate hacking specialists are typically Certified Ethical Hackers who are procured to counteract any potential risk to the PC security framework or system. Courses for Ethical hacking have turned out to be generally well known and many are taking it up as a genuine calling. Ethical hacking courses have assembled tremendous reactions everywhere throughout the world.

Do you need your business to have a protected framework? Shield it from questionable characters who need to take delicate archives by enlisting a legitimate data security expert. They can give Ethical hacking, infiltration testing, and Payment Card Industry (PCI) preparing and counseling. Here is more data about what this is and what it can accomplish for your organization.

Another expression for a data security pro is a PC security authority. This master is in charge of shielding the PC framework from dangers. These dangers can be inward or outside in nature. Other than, private organizations, the expert gives administrations to government offices and instructive foundations.

The requirement for these gifted experts keeps on developing. This is on the grounds that dangers to PC frameworks and systems grow quickly alongside mechanical improvements. Because of this, the authority must keep on overhauling their degree of learning. The individual in question should likewise expand armory of helpful apparatuses, applications, and frameworks.

A fundamental safety effort includes the control of passwords. A PC security master may require the individuals from the organization to change their secret key often. This diminishes the odds of unapproved access to secret projects, systems, or databases.

Who might I shield my business from?

Ordinarily, the most risky hazard to any PC system originates from outside sources. The authority sets up firewalls for programmers. The individual consistently introduces programs that have programmed cautions when there is any endeavor to penetrate the framework. You can even discover cutting edge programs that can call attention to where the programmer is by distinguishing the web convention address of the interloper.

Two famous administrations offered by PC masters are moral hacking and infiltration testing.

Moral hacking and Penetration testing 101

Gifted PC specialists more often than not perform moral hacking. They utilize their programming abilities to know the shortcomings in PC frameworks. While you can discover non-moral programmers manhandling the vulnerabilities for individual addition, the moral programmer assesses and calls attention to out, at that point recommends changes to fortify the framework. PC specialists guard frameworks and data with their moral hacking administrations.

Most IT pros consider moral hacking as plain hacking in light of the fact that regardless it utilizes learning of PC frameworks trying to crash or enter them. Most entrepreneurs think of it as moral in light of its motivation, which is to build the security in frameworks.

Penetration testing, then again, is a sort of security assessment done on a PC framework. This includes an individual attempting to hack into the framework. The objective of this administration is to see whether somebody with malignant goal can enter the framework. Infiltration testing can uncover what projects or applications programmers can get to once they enter the framework. There are numerous organizations and online organizations offering infiltration testing. This is exceptionally prescribed, as harm to a PC framework brought about by a threatening assault can be expensive to fix.

Most organizations are required to have penetration testing. Consistence with the standard can appear to be troublesome from the outset, however you can discover numerous organizations that have enough involvement to enable organizations to meet the prerequisites at all levels.

CHAPTER THREE

How the process of hacking works

PC hacking is the act of causing malignant alterations to a program so as to accomplish an objective outside the first motivation behind the maker. An individual who draws in into these exercises is known as a Hacker, who is normally a specialist developer who views hacking as a workmanship and as an approach to apply their aptitudes, all things considered, circumstances. Be that as it may, different programmers have definitely more risky goals than just to exhibit their aptitudes, such as taking individual data, increasing unapproved get to, and so on.

Who are Hackers?

Hacking has been a significant issue. Hacking has increased huge improvement after the presentation of the web in view of the simple entry to frameworks around the globe which this innovation gives. With the expanding utilization of the web, hacking has likewise turned into a progressively major issue as of late. Programmers are typically youthful people in the field of programming yet there are likewise some old sheep. Likewise the simple access to a data has extended ability in the field of hacking. Presently it doesn't require a specialist software engineer to hack a PC of private system. Only a decent directing book can transform a child into a specialist programmer.

Dangers of Hacking

Programmers have turned out to be master to the point that even goliath programming partners like Microsoft and Nintendo are not protected from this wretchedness, causing misfortunes of a huge number of dollars consistently. The objectives are not constrained to the goliaths, private clients are likewise significantly influenced by this risk. The burglary of individual data, credit demolition, and unapproved access to private data are just a portion of the dangers that hacking posture to private clients.

The most effective method to ensure yourself against Hacking

Hacking is an unpredictable issue however the procedure of to shield yourself from hacking is very straightforward. Basic safety measures can mean the contrast between a full verification secure framework and a helpless system. Pursue these straightforward tips to spare yourself from programmers.

Programmers are continually looking for remaining details in your security. So its critical to focus on every single seemingly insignificant detail so as to have a full confirmation security for your information and PC. Infection and Spyware are genuine Hacker's devices. Debilitating your security and covertly sending your private data in wrong hands. The most ideal approach to beat them is to utilize hostile to infection and against spyware programming. It is additionally imperative to utilize refreshed renditions of security programming and OS as they loses adequacy with time. Another great technique is to utilize a Firewall to stop unapproved access to your framework. What's more, it is likewise imperative to be cautious when surfing the web and utilizing messages. These straightforward stunts can mean the distinction. Also, recollect, Care is Better Than Cure.

At the point when individuals initially catch wind of hacking, they will ordinarily consider this to be as something negative. In fact, hacking has consistently been tied in with exploiting unprotected or feebly monitored locales or frameworks for the people claim narrow minded intrigue. Along these lines, others (regularly organizations,) who need to reinforce the security of their online frameworks go to experts for assistance. These expert programmers (in some cases known as "white caps,") utilize a moral hacking system to help assemble a more grounded resistance against genuine hacking dangers. By purposely "assaulting" the framework, they can rapidly recognize its blemishes, and after that start to think of emergency courses of action to slow down, keep away from or dispose of genuine real hacking assaults.

From the moral hacking technique, you can see that not all hacks are awful. The demonstration of hacking morally into a framework so as to uncover conceivable frail focuses, ones that genuine programmers, or "dark caps" (because of less flavorful aims) can misuse, can help keep the organization from loss of income or notoriety. Without a doubt, a great deal of organizations are presently looking for the administrations of the individuals who can play out this undertaking since they comprehend that the best way to battle against gifted programmers is with another talented programmer of their own!

Those with a solid comprehension of PC frameworks can prepare to complete these administrations. In spite of the fact that when you consider the moral hacking technique incorporates breaking into online frameworks, it is very conceivable that many white caps today have picked up their encounters initially as dark caps themselves!

Insofar as your activities have been allowed by the organization who claims the framework, the underhandedness or turmoil that you'll make during the hacking procedure will altogether profit the organization inasmuch as they development and dispose of those shortcomings.

Moral programmers are either procured experts who have become famous as dark cap programmers, or are genuine workers of the organization who are educated enough to play out the errand.

This isn't about positive or negative programmers, white caps or dark caps; eventually it is about the advantage of the organization, and the insurance of touchy information they may hold. On the off chance that you had a less attractive past (dark cap,) however have since chosen to work for the framework than against it, you will be all around thought about in view of the administration you would now be able to give.

The moral hacking technique is tied in with getting results with regards to ensuring on the web frameworks against ruinous assaults. You are concerned uniquely with guarding the benefits and interests, and just by deduction and acting like a genuine programmer would this be able to be accomplished.

Doubtlessly, this is a successful method to shield from online dangers. In case you're an organization, don't waver to contract a white cap programmer, since they are furnished with the correct information and aptitudes to battle a danger from another programmer. Then again, in case you're associated with hacking yourself, maybe there would be a profession for you to consider in chipping away at the opposite side?

PC hacking is characterized as any demonstration of getting to a PC or PC arrange without the proprietor's authorization. At times, hacking requires breaking firewalls or secret phrase assurances to obtain entrance. In different cases, an individual may hack into a PC that has few or no barriers. Regardless of whether there are no protections to "break" through, just accessing a PC and its data qualifies as criminal PC hacking.

To be sentenced for PC hacking, it must be demonstrated that the respondent intentionally accessed a PC with the goal of rupturing without consent. In some cases people, especially youthful PC keen young people, break in to a PC or system just to demonstrate that they can. They may boast about their achievement a short time later, utilizing the trick to parade their PC capacities. Despite the fact that there might not have been an aim to take or dupe from the hacked framework, the litigant can in any case be criminally charged.

At the point when an individual is captured in Florida for hacking, the person will be accused of a lawful offense. On the off chance that the respondent got to a PC framework without approval however did not plan to take or dupe, the individual will be accused of a third degree lawful offense. Assuming, be that as it may, the programmer broke into the framework and intended to cheat the proprietor of cash or data, the person will be accused of a second degree lawful offense. Past PC hacking offenses have included endeavors to take charge card data, standardized savings numbers, or touchy organization or government data.

PC hacking is viewed as a noteworthy danger to organization honesty, government classification, and individual security. It is thusly arraigned forcefully in a courtroom. Under Florida law, a third degree lawful offense for hacking can bring about a greatest multi year jail sentence and up to $5,000 in fines. For a hacking offense that includes robbery or fake movement, the respondent could be punished with as long as 15 years in jail and a $10,000 fine.

Past the quick court requested punishments, a hacking offense can annihilate a person's close to home and expert notoriety. The person in question may experience inconvenience applying to schools, acquiring grants, getting a new line of work, or getting an advance. Indeed, even numerous years after your conviction, you could at present be adversely influenced by your lawful offense PC hacking charge.

The principle asset programmers depend upon, aside from their very own resourcefulness, is PC code. While there is an enormous network of programmers on the Internet, just a generally modest number of programmers really program code. Numerous programmers search out and download code composed by other individuals. There are a large number of various projects programmers use to investigate PCs and systems. These projects give programmers a great deal of control over honest clients and associations - when a gifted programmer realizes how a framework functions, he can configuration programs that adventure it.

Malignant programmers use projects to:

• Log keystrokes: Some projects enable programmers to audit each keystroke a PC client makes. Once introduced on an injured individual's PC, the projects record every keystroke, giving the programmer all that he needs to penetrate a framework or even take somebody's personality.

• Hack passwords: There are numerous approaches to hack somebody's secret word, from instructed theories to straightforward calculations that produce mixes of letters, numbers and images. The experimentation technique for hacking passwords is known as a savage power assault, which means the programmer attempts to create each conceivable mix to obtain entrance. Another approach to hack passwords is to utilize a lexicon assault, a program that supplements regular words into secret phrase fields.

• Infect a PC or framework with an infection: Computer infections are projects intended to copy themselves and cause issues extending from smashing a PC to clearing out everything on a framework's hard drive. A programmer may introduce an infection by penetrating a framework, however it's significantly more typical for programmers to make basic infections and send them out to potential exploited people through email, texts, Web locales with downloadable substance or distributed systems.

•   Gain secondary passage get to: Similar to hacking passwords, a few programmers make programs that quest for unprotected pathways into system frameworks and PCs. In the beginning of the Internet, numerous PC frameworks had constrained security, making it feasible for a programmer to discover a pathway into the framework without a username or secret word. Another way a programmer may pick up secondary passage access is to taint a PC or framework with a Trojan steed.

•   Create zombie PCs: A zombie PC, or bot, is a PC that a programmer can use to send spam or submit Distributed Denial of Service (DDoS) assaults. After an injured individual executes apparently blameless code, an association opens between his PC and the programmer's framework. The programmer can covertly control the unfortunate casualty's PC, utilizing it to carry out wrongdoings or spread spam.

• Spy on email: Hackers have made code that allows them to catch and peruse email messages - the Internet's identical to wiretapping. Today, most email projects use encryption equations so perplexing that regardless of whether a programmer catches the message, he won't probably read it.

Enthusiasm or Madness: Now days, it has turned into an energy to find out about hacking and data security. In some cases I don't comprehend that whether it is an energy or a sort of franticness. This energy has come about because of a few news stories, media stories and the fervor demonstrating hacking related excites in movies. Be that as it may, then again there is a reality additionally that not very many people groups know anything top to bottom about the point of hacking and data security. In this way, I would recommend that without satisfactory learning kindly don't get frantic behind energy. Once in a while this energy may end up hazardous from the legitimate perspective. There is nothing incorrectly to pick up ability, yet there is have to understand a reality about off base issues behind hacking. I will result in these present circumstances theme inside and out, later in a similar part.

Be Alert and Aware: Do you feel that hacking is a specialist level work? Do you imagine that data security and hacking would one say one are and same things? On the off chance that yes! At that point you are completely off-base. Numerous youngsters in the age gathering of 14-16 years are having adequate information to hack any site or gather significant information certainties from the web. Along these lines, web being the enormous wellspring of data it's a tyke game to perform hacking related exercises. Numerous programmers whose point is to simply acquire cash from you, they give courses and workshops alongside mislead you that, "master hacking in a moral manner for a splendid vocation". Be that as it may, I am not going to clarify along these lines, to any of you. Rather, I might want to clarify the reality in a positive manner with an inspirational frame of mind. An educator's undertaking is to show right way to understudies and not mislead them for picking up their own advantages. So I would propose that as opposed to going for the information of hacking, gain the learning by picking up something, which is said to be a specialist level employment. What's more, this master level employment is known as data security mastery in specialized terms. Expectation you may have comprehended the contrast between hacking (not master level occupation) and data security (master level employment) from this point. Along these lines, be alert from such misguidance.

Other then energy, one progressively side of coin likewise exists. Numerous foundations and free people groups call themselves programmer as well as data security specialists. In any case, the truth behind their mastery and aptitudes gets showed before non-specialized people groups and the unfortunate casualties who experience for preparing, courses, confirmations, classes and workshop with such kinds of self-asserted programmers or organizations, when such exploited people and non-specialized people groups understand that they are not fulfilled for which they have invested energy and cash. The genuine reality behind tricking is that the people groups who experience for such classes, workshops, courses, and so on most likely experience through a brain research that, "the individual or foundation from which we will get information during the instructional meetings is a specialist or is giving quality training as he was distributed by media offices or that it's a marked name in market for related subject ability or that he is a writer of any book". I have confidence in handy, official and those assignments or activities for which proof lies before my eyes. Along these lines, I am attempting to disclose to everybody that consistently be alert and mindful, with the goal that your scarcely earned pay does not get spend in such pointless exercise in futility.

Any individual keen on distributing any information on the Internet requires Web Hosting. Web facilitating has been around for quite a long while now and has advanced from straightforward HTML pages facilitating, little basic locales with a couple of pictures into out and out online facilitated applications where end clients can visit a webpage, associate with the site proprietor, and even buy merchandise and enterprises everywhere throughout the web.

The utilization of Internet as a mechanism for coordinating business over the globe with the assistance of Web Based programming applications has created wide scope of online innovations like ASP, ASP.NET, JSP, PHP, and others. This decision has constrained different choices for web facilitating now as HTML put together destinations work similarly well with respect to both Linux and Windows stages.

Web facilitating stages change from various kinds of working frameworks. Microsoft Windows Server and Redhat Linux are only two models and likely the most notable web facilitating stages. Along these lines, what is Windows or Linux web facilitating and what are the favorable circumstances and detriments to facilitating your site on either Server. What's more, why now Linux is increasing greater ubiquity. All things considered, that is only the appropriate response would it say it isn't?

Linux stage has been created by Community based endeavors and it has been rendered for expert use with the endeavors of numerous IT organizations like Red Hat, Suse, Mandrake, and like. This foundation of Community advancement and open source nature of Linux Server and reinforcement of expert IT organizations has made Linux stage all the more dominant, modest and verified.

The cost adequacy in this focused period is a

noteworthy lift that the organizations required without settling on the quality and security of the item. Aside from ASP, ASP.NET, all other real online advances function admirably with Linux. The for all intents and purposes free dissemination of PHP, MySQL, PERL has diminished the expenses of the site facilitating colossally on Linux Server. At Sakshay, we give both sort of facilitating administrations yet the guidance to organizations requiring Hacking for HTML based sites, little applications like Recipe site is to utilize Linux Hosting.

The danger of infections, spamming and hacking is additionally very less with Linux Hosting. Right off the bat, this is because of the strong engineering of Linux Server and Secondly, because of many savvy programming projects accessible for insurance on Linux Platform.

Coming up next are the benefits of utilizing Linux based web server contrasted with Windows based web server:

Steady and Robust: Linux/Unix working frameworks has customarily been accepted to be entirely steady and vigorous. A site housed on a Linux working framework will have high up-time (of the request for 99.9%). Obviously, different factors, for example, control supply, arrange administrator abilities, and system load and so forth additionally matter with regards to keeping up the framework uptime.

Minimal effort of proprietorship: The Linux OS comes free of expense (or at inconsequential cost, for the most part cost of conveyance). Likewise, it has undeniable server, and work area applications that comes free alongside the OS. These server applications, (for example, FTP, Web Server, DNS Server, File Server and so on.) being free, are additionally entirely steady.

Easy to understand: When it comes to web facilitating, it is anything but difficult to have on

Linux web servers. The way toward transferring and facilitating is practically same for both Linux and Windows web servers. In the event that you need to utilize a Windows based instrument, for example,

Simple to move between hosts: A site intended to be facilitated on a Linux based web server can be facilitated on a Windows web server effectively, where as the switch isn't in every case genuine.

Most generally utilized: Linux/Unix based web facilitating is most broadly utilized contrasted with Windows based web facilitating.

Versatility: Scalability and future extension are other real criteria to consider while facilitating an application. A site is dynamic. Typically, a site begins with a couple of pages of html and develops over some undefined time frame to suit the clients prerequisites. It is desirable over structure a site remembering this necessities. A site intended for similarity with a Linux/Unix based web server meets the versatility prerequisite effectively without making any webpage wide plan changes.

Self Management of your site on a Linux Web Hacking Plan with Sakshay facilitating is made simple with our Implementation of the Award Winning Control Panel programming by Sw-Soft called Plesk. Plesk is an electronic interface to your Linux web facilitating account that enables you to make email addresses and letter drops, see your site traffic insights, set authorizations on your HTML, PHP pages, MySQL, and that's only the tip of the iceberg. We likewise furnish Windows Hacking with Plesk Panel.

I will give you my very own model here! I have a few books about me in different papers and media organizations, however this doesn't imply that I am demonstrating to you the correct way or that I am a specialist. For instance might be conceivable that I am a programmer, however this does not demonstrate that I am a specialist. Along these lines, master level occupation is an entirely unexpected issue. The clarification about contrast among hacking and aptitude will come in next sections So, first look at the degree of my insight, how much for all intents and purposes I am ready to demonstrate my mastery, regardless of whether I am legitimate and lawful while experiencing for such undertakings lastly the proof part that whatever activities I attempt are demonstrated directly before eyes, rather than simply talking hypothetically. Continuously affirm yourself first, that you are learning with ideal individual or foundation or simply burning through your time and cash. May be conceivable that people groups may get charges from you and thusly give you the learning of something(any other subject or point about data innovation field), which isn't single percent part of hacking or data security related themes. This happens most presumably with non-specialized people groups or fresher in data innovation field.

False Publicity: Secondly, affirm that you are in any event picking up the learning up to a level for which you have paid a specific sum. Don't simply go behind false exposures before you affirm yourself and your inward emotions state that you are proceeding onward right way. As worries to book distributers, media organizations and movies, I might want to affirm that none of them may have full and fledge specialized learning about data security field as worries as far as anyone is concerned. It's like after models on me:

An individual comes and reveals to me that you are a specialist please propose me a few medications which can kill my genuine infection of malignancy. I am a specialized proficient and not an organic expert who will tackle this issue.

An individual comes and reveals to me that recommend a decent legal advisor who can safeguard my case in court. Presently reveal to me how would I give recommendation regarding which legal advisor can demonstrate this individual honest in official courtroom.

Along these lines, I can't do anything or have any learning about any field which isn't my subject or zone of work. So also, even media people groups, book distributers and movie producers does not have sufficient or complete information and they accept the announcement to be genuine which is disclosed to them by many misleading self-asserted programmers and additionally rumored establishments. Along these lines, these people groups are likewise not in charge of a portion of these sorts of exercises distributed by them on any medium.

Language Troubling: There is one all the more piece of deceiving called utilization of futile and confounded language so as to misinform understudies and particularly actually stable experts. This is a smart piece of trick utilized by numerous self guaranteed security people groups to mislead others. Typically when any self asserted programmer or foundation knows nothing about convoluted or master level point, and in such circumstance they need to incorporate master level subjects in their investigation material without having any master level information; such people groups utilize extremely muddled expressions of English and set up the substance in such a way, that it turns out to be exceptionally hard to see notwithstanding for the people who are familiar with English. An exceptionally confounded coding and pointless specialized terms are utilized in their examination material, with the goal that the exploited people can't comprehend or guarantee against such self asserted programmers thus called particular organizations, in a legitimate way. At the point when any unfortunate casualty (client of such material) experiences such investigation materials and courses just as affirmations, they become powerless to see such entangled and misleading language, topped off of futile and non-justifiable specialized terms. Presently, when they don't comprehend anything the basic brain research of such exploited people gets that, "it's a piece of master level work and that is the reason they can't comprehend the issue or that he won't almost certainly complete this activity effectively as he isn't gifted, etc. Along these lines, the exploited people think themselves in charge of not understanding the master level work. Be that as it may, they don't have the foggiest idea about that they have never been shown anything, which can be called a specialist level training or employment. This is the thing that I am attempting to clarify you that it

Some of the time the Print Server is an element or an administration on another gadget, for example, a switch or remote passageway. This is a smart thought however has various hindrances, in particular the way that the printing capacity is simply one more capacity on the switch and it may not give a similar degree of administration as committed print servers do.

Print servers more often than not have an administration interface that can regularly be gotten to over the system itself. This interface will now and again enable the manager of the server to set up client consents and to set up a particular activity of the gadget. A client can possibly get to a particular printer when it has been approved by methods for some verification strategy. At the point when numerous printers are being used, the server can be customized with the goal that a few clients may just get to specific printers while others may have consent to get to all printers. Having different printers connected to the print server can likewise give strength in case of a printer breaking down, the clients can either be coordinated to utilize another printer or can physically choose another printing gadget.

With versatility being a major piece of systems administration nowadays, and remote systems administration being very typical, having a remote empowered print server bodes well. Clients can get to the server legitimately over the remote system, subject to a similar authorisation and confirmation as required by a wired gadget. It additionally implies that the remote print server can be found anyplace, if it is in scope of the system remote passage or remote switch that is the center point of the system. The printers themselves will typically be associated with remote print servers by means of a USB Cable, which gives the network, yet sometimes can likewise be utilized to control the printer. The server could associate remotely to the passage or switch or could be associated by a length of Ethernet link.

A Wireless empowered Server giving printer sharing should have arrange certifications simply like some other gadget on a remote system, at the end of the day a SSID will be required just as any verification and encryption settings. Any customer PCs will be required to have the printer programming introduced to permit all print capacities to be accessible.

As organizations are depending on PCs and most recent innovation apparatuses it is critical to make them screen gadgets and assignments that can make the system up and easily running. In a private company arrange there might be at least two machines associated with one another connecting with a server. Another significant thing is that the server must be sound at all the occasions to keep the business procedure smooth and fine.

For these reasons a legitimate server checking equipment is predominantly required by each association. These are taken care of by experienced and productive architects and furthermore the establishment of these is simple. Any individual having some specialized 'know how' can introduce these. They don't require especially IT backing and they begin to screen the system and keep it up at all the occasions. At the same time its product likewise keeps the system defended against various noxious and devilish clients who consistently attempt to enter the system to take the business information. It is the obligation of solid observing programming to check the machines and system occasionally and guarantee the security of the business data.

The valid statement here is if the equipment or

programming projects quit working they send a caution to the server about this. Since your IT framework is the foundation of the whole business process so it must not be bothered by any inconsistency or specialized issue. While organizing the checking equipment or programming need must be to affirm that it underpins the system for which it is being taken. Similarity ought to be coordinated to the server as the exhibition relies upon the correct kind of equipment. It is exceptionally pivotal to proactively screen the issue before it makes vacations and may stop the procedure affecting the business.

The issues can occur at any area on the server like on the focal handling unit or on the memory consequently the screen program ought to be keen enough to examine the main driver of the issue. Something else that makes the server the executives solid is the examination between the past reports with the enhanced one by which the server execution efficiency can be resolved. The reports produced by it ought to be in great arrangements and can be framed in the graphical structure whenever required. The cautions must be proactive to send the data to the client before it hurts the procedure. With every one of these things there are different advantages to have these projects might be again talked about in the following part.

Botnets have turned out to be progressively predominant as malware journalists turns out to be increasingly advanced. One of the more malicious bits of malware that appeared in 2008 is called Mebroot. This infection, which is still in the wild today, is a rootkit that changes a PCs Master Boot Record enabling it to introduce even before the working arrangement of the PC gets stacked, which shields it from against infection insurance programming.

When organizing components of big business arrange security, counteracting malware like a rootkit that conceals itself and takes into account all out control of the machine is directly at the top. Mebroot without anyone else is generally innocuous since it doesn't contain a particular applications however turns into a stage for other malware. The most common of these is Torpig, an enormous botnet.

Torpig contains various information taking components of malware that output the contaminated machine for private information, records and passwords just as far as anyone knows allowing assailants full access to the PC. In 2009 a group of specialists had the option to assume responsibility for the Torpig botnet for ten days. During that time, they hauled out over 70GB of stolen data from contaminated PCs.

Mebroot gets onto PCs by a client heading off to a site utilizing an internet browser that is more seasoned and has not been fixed to wipe out the shortcomings that Mebroot uses to add itself to the client's framework. A surefire approach to identify Mebroot is with a system based identifier, since the infection conceals itself on the machine it is introduced on which may make it imperceptible.

Just some infection scanners can discover and evacuate Mebroot. On the off chance that a machine is rebooting or acting tainted, yet no infection appears in an output, fixing the Master Boot Record on the framework will evacuate Mebroot on the off chance that it introduced. Doing a web look for "Fix MBR" will turn up a couple of various approaches to fix the Master Boot Record. After that is done, run a total infection filter on the PC again to find anything extra that was covered up.

The best strategy is to avoid machine disease is by keeping programs refreshed, and working both host and system based malware discovery programs that are continually refreshed with constant data to stop any contamination before it begins.

System Control is a phony security program which will commonly download onto Windows PCs and after that endeavor to fool you into downloading the bogus move up to the program. In spite of the fact that it might appear as though this product apparatus is giving you an authentic administration, the truth of the matter is that it's sitting idle however faking the checking of your framework so as to get you to purchase the updated programming of the program and to take your own subtleties. In the event that you are unfortunate enough to have this contamination, it's suggested that you evacuate it in the most complete manner conceivable, by utilizing the instructional exercise illustrated underneath...

The Network Control program is known as "malware" (vindictive programming), which will essentially introduce onto your PC and after that work to play out a progression of terrible things on your PC. There are an enormous number of these bogus projects being moved around the Internet through any semblance of Trojan Horse infections, counterfeit email connections and false antivirus checks on the web. In spite of the fact that this infection may appear to be accommodating, the truth of the matter is that will be that it's constantly working out of sight of your PC to take your own subtleties and cause an enormous measure of harm. In the event that you need to dispose of this infection, you should most likely utilize the right methods which will dispose of all the potential harm it might have.

The best approach to dispose of Network Control is to totally expel every one of the components it has - from the phony application you find in the forefront to the various phony documents that are working in the "foundation". Numerous individuals feel that this infection simply has the bogus application as its principle issue - and thusly attempt and evacuate it by erasing the records this program requires to run (you can see the documents recorded beneath). In any case, this technique for expulsion will just lead your PC into a greater arrangement of issues, as the concealed codes this infection implants onto your PC won't just draw in different infections to the framework, yet will likewise invest considerably more energy to take your own subtleties. This implies in the event that you need to totally expel Network Control from your PC, and make it keep running as easily as conceivable once more, you should hope to utilize a computerized evacuation device which will dispose of all pieces of this infection for good.

The documents this program uses are in this catalog:

* c:\NetworkControl\

To evacuate this infection, you first should probably utilize a "malware expulsion device" called XoftSpy. There are various malware evacuation programs accessible which will dispose of Network Control, yet our experience has discovered that the Canadian-created XoftSpy is the best and solid apparatus to expel it with. This program has been planned by an enormous PC security

Working with Kali Linux

Is it accurate to say that you are new to Linux or considering utilizing it just because? Hang on! What the hell I'm stating here! There's no word called " New to Linux" or " first time Linux client". Without your cognizant, you presumably use it each and every day! What's more, you were thinking Linux implied for the programming geeks, programmers and experiencing Linux means utilizing that great old green terminal!

That is bigot you know!!

The primary inquiry ought to be-would you say you are new to individual Linux processing?

Well in the event that your answer is "Yes", at that point stress not, a better working framework is prepared than be served for his solitary ace. See what I did there? If not, I intend to state that you and just YOU are the proprietors of your equipment and programming. Nobody going to introduce some horrible application that you don't need or change the framework setting while you are getting a charge out of good old " amusing kitty video" on the web!

In the realm of Linux individualized computing, there is a plenty of decision to look over. Individuals from Linux planet call this "Dispersions". This means, while the essential framework 'Bit' is indistinguishable, the look and believe and the whole biological system can be unique.

My undisputed top choice, for my everyday work area work in any event, is Kali Linux. It is a Debian-determined Linux circulation intended for computerized legal sciences and infiltration testing. In any case, for my own utilization, I lean toward Linux Mint or Elementary OS. In any case, here are some others you may have known about:

1.   Fedora

2.   Zorin

3.   openSUSE

4.   Debian

Those are the greatest dispersion as far as clients. Be that as it may, as a tenderfoot, you should utilize " Linux Mint cinnamon version". It intently looks like your windows PC and on the off chance that you are originating from the universe of natural product, I will propose giving an attempt to the "Basic OS" or "Deepin OS". They intently look like the Mac biological system.

Stick with Linux Mint: From the main day of relocation, it is prescribed that you stick with appropriations like Linux Mint, Zorin, Linux Lite e.t.c. There are anything but difficult to introduce and utilize and they have an immense number of online client base. These clients are genuinely proficient and kind, ask them what issue you are confronting and you will include the right answer inside hours if not inside minutes! Linux Mint accompanies genuinely respectable programming out of the case. This incorporates libre office (a free and open source office suite), Thunderbird (Email customer), Rhythm (Music Player) and Firefox(you can without much of a stretch introduce chrome and chromium). As you get to acquainted with Linux condition, you may wind up exploring different avenues regarding diverse distros and DE (Desktop Environment), be that as it may, until further notice, it is a smart thought to stay with Linux

Mint and gradually seeing how Linux functions.

Inundate Yourself: Best approach to set an association with Linux is to make it your day by day driver. Most assuredly the initial couple of day's rides would be rough and unusual, so is everything new and past one's customary range of familiarity. A dissemination like Linux Mint, Zorin and Ubuntu attempt to make the adventure from Windows or Mac into the universe of Linux smooth and enchanted! Really soon I can guarantee you that you will ask why you at any point utilized something besides Linux!

Try not to be frightened of the terminal: Distributions like Ubuntu and Linux Mint are made with the goal that you never truly need to open the terminal direction line on the off chance that you would prefer not to. Be that as it may, becoming more acquainted with the direction line is significantly empowered, and it's not so difficult as it takes a gander from the start. The direction line is truly preferred and increasingly profitable over the Graphical User Interface (GUI) much of the time. What takes a few ticks, parchments, keystrokes, and more snaps in the GUI can ordinarily be cultivated with a solitary terminal order. That is the straightforwardness!

Make a coalition with Google: With the progressing time, you will go over something in Linux that you want to do, be that as it may, aren't sure what strategy you ought to pursue. This is the place Google will turn into your best mate! In the event that there's something you can't make sense of how to do in Linux, somebody other than you has kept running into that equivalent issue previously. The authority Ubuntu Wiki and AskUbuntu gatherings will obviously be controlling your hunt results. Advantageously, Linux Mint is based on Ubuntu, so whatever arrangement works in Ubuntu is for all intents and purposes ensured to work in Linux Mint also.

There's significantly more I need to state, nonetheless, I figure you will learn them in the end. In the end, I might want to express that pursue Linux blog pages, pursue their web based life. Think about subjects and symbol packs and consistently want for exploring new territory and imaginative. Have a glad an adventure to the wonderland.

CHAPTER FOUR

Let's start! How to install the kali linux

Introducing Kali Linux on your PC is a simple procedure. To begin with, you'll need perfect PC equipment. The equipment prerequisites are insignificant as recorded beneath, however better equipment will normally give better execution. The i386 pictures have a default PAE bit, so you can run them on frameworks with over 4GB of RAM. Download Kali Linux and either copy the ISO to DVD, or set up a USB stick with Kali Linux Live as the establishment medium.

Establishment Prerequisites

•	A least of 20 GB plate space for the Kali Linux introduce.

•   RAM for i386 and amd64 designs, least: 1GB, suggested: 2GB or more.

•   CD-DVD Drive/USB boot support

Getting ready for the Installation

1.   Download Kali linux.

2.   Burn The Kali linux ISO to DVD or Image Kali Linux Live to USB.

3.   Ensure that your PC is set to boot from CD/USB in your BIOS.

Kali Linux Installation Procedure

1.   To begin your establishment, boot with your picked establishment medium. You ought to be welcomed with the Kali Linux boot menu. Pick a Graphical or a Text-Mode introduce. In this model, we picked a GUI introduce.

2.   Select your favored language and after that your nation area. You'll additionally be provoked to arrange your console with the fitting keymap.

3.   The installer will duplicate the picture to your hard circle, test your system interfaces, and after that brief you to enter a hostname for your framework. In the model underneath, we've entered "kali" as the hostname.

4.   Enter a powerful secret phrase for the root account.

5.   Next, set your time zone.

6.   The installer will currently test your circles and offer you four decisions. For an Encrypted LVM introduce, pick the "Guided – go through whole circle and set scrambled LVM" alternative as demonstrated as follows.

7.   Choose the goal drive to introduce Kali. For this situation, we picked a USB drive goal. We will utilize this USB drive to boot a scrambled example of Kali.

8.   Confirm your parceling plan and proceed with the establishment.

9.   Next, you will be requested an encryption secret word. You should recollect this secret phrase and use it each opportunity to boot the scrambled occurrence of Kali Linux.

10.   Configure system mirrors. Kali utilizes a focal storehouse to circulate applications. You'll have to enter any proper intermediary data as required.

11.   Next, introduce GRUB.

12.   Finally, click Continue to reboot into your new Kali establishment. On the off chance that you utilized a USB gadget as a goal drive, ensure you empower booting from USB gadgets in your BIOS. You will be requested the encryption secret word you set before on each boot.

Since you've finished introducing Kali Linux, it's a great opportunity to alter your framework. This digital book part has more data and you can likewise discover tips on the best way to benefit from Kali in our User Forums.

Digital security is surely the most pivotal part as the entirety of your framework requires is significant guard dog programming and a firewall insurance framework. Consistently, the explanations for system security are Trojans and key lumberjacks; these undermining projects enter one's framework without your assent through illegal locales visited by clients, in this way making the issues that pursue. Inability to secure your PCs may mean an inability to ensure your business character, which may at last rush an individual towards calamity.

In the no so distant past, firewalls were the restrictive area of organizations, intended to shield their PCs from unapproved access by contenders, displeased workers, etc. These days, in any case, despite the fact that firewalls stay a key piece of corporate systems, they've made consistent advances into the universe of home processing.

There are numerous explanations behind the changing job of firewalls, including falling costs, less complex structures and more prominent needs. The early firewalls were fundamentally equipment based gadgets, and they were over the top expensive also. At the point when programming put together firewalls originally accompanied respect to the market, they were confounded to utilize and very exorbitant too. Nowadays, notwithstanding, there are various reasonable, and even free, programming put together firewalls with respect to the market. Truly, firewalls have turned out to be so well known and significant that Microsoft incorporated a free one as a component of its Windows XP Service Pack 2 update.

There are numerous reasons why a home PC client needs to utilize a firewall. For a certain something, the individuals who interface with their office system should have a firewall set up to anticipate unapproved access to the home PC and the corporate system. What's more, anybody with a fast Internet association will get themselves the subject of undesirable consideration by programmers, infection/spyware authors, etc. A firewall can help hinder that undesirable traffic.

Why you need the security of a firewall

The truth of the matter is that a PC which is unprotected by a firewall can be hacked in merely minutes, by any of various robotized programmer programs that meander the Internet. The main way you can make certain that your PC and the data it contains are sheltered is to ensure it with a firewall.

From multiple points of view, running a PC loaded with individual data without the insurance of a firewall resembles leaving your vehicle entryways opened with the keys in the start. It's similarly as simple for an Internet criminal to take the data from your PC for what it's worth for a cheat to take your vehicle. Truth be told, taking the data on your PC would presumably be significantly simpler.

Along these lines, similarly as you ought to secure your vehicle by locking the entryways, you should secure your PC with a dependable firewall. A firewall program, related to against infection programming, hostile to spyware programs and other Internet assurance, gives a safe and safe figuring condition for you and your family.

Be that as it may, it's imperative to download and introduce all the fundamental updates to your working framework before introducing any sort of firewall program. This is on the grounds that a product based firewall would itself be able to be in danger if the working framework has a security defect.

What's more, it's constantly a smart thought to stay up with the latest, as there are in every case new security dangers, and security defects, being found. So having your working framework cutting-edge will give you a decent base to pass by.

Finding a dependable firewall

There are various superb firewall programs available, and it's commonly a smart thought to attempt a few of them before choosing which one to utilize. Look at the online surveys and after that since most firewalls give a free time for testing, exploit this choice before you purchase.

A few firewalls will come bundled with other security situated programming, for example, hostile to infection programming or spyware end programs. Other firewall projects are essentially independent items. Whichever type you pick is more a matter of individual inclination than all else. In any case, regardless of what sort of firewall you pick, it's critical to arrange it appropriately, as indicated by the directions gave. An appropriately arranged firewall, related to great enemy of infection programming and a spyware disposal program, is the most ideal approach to ensure your PC and the important information that it contains.

Normal idea

This section portrays basic idea of Windows individual firewalls. It isn't important to execute the firewall along these lines to have it secure. Normal individual firewall is actualized as three or four separate parts.

Bit driver

The initial segment is piece driver. Its has two principle capacities and that is the reason it is now and again actualized in two parts as opposed to in one. The primary capacity is a parcel channel. As a rule on the NDIS, TDI or the two levels this driver checks each bundle that roll in from the system or goes out to the system. This is otherwise called inbound and outbound association security.

CHAPTER FIVE

How to scan network

Nmap, short for **Network Mapper**, is a tool used by many security professionals all over the world.

The utility works in both Linux and Windows and is command line (CLI) driven. However for those a little more timid of the command line, there is a wonderful graphical frontend for nmap called **zenmap**.

It is strongly recommended that individuals learn the CLI version of nmap as it provides much more flexibility when compared to the zenmap graphical edition.

What reason does nmap server? Incredible inquiry. Nmap takes into consideration a chairman to rapidly and altogether find out about the frameworks on a system, thus the name, Network MAPper or nmap.

Nmap can rapidly find live has just as administrations related with that have. Nmap's usefulness can be broadened much further with the Nmap Scripting Engine, regularly condensed as NSE.

This scripting motor enables directors to rapidly make a content that can be utilized to decide whether a newfound helplessness exists on their system. Numerous contents have been created and included with most nmap introduces.

An expression of alert – nmap is a generally utilized by individuals with both great and awful expectations. Outrageous alert ought to be taken to guarantee that you aren't utilizing nmap against frameworks that consent has not be expressly given in a composed/legitimate understanding. Kindly use alert when utilizing the nmap apparatus.

Arranging a remote system includes setting up a remote switch or passageway and introducing remote connectors on the organized PCs. The remote switch must be set in a focal area in light of the fact that the PCs closer to the switch or passage acquire quicker system speeds. The remote switch should be associated with a power source and a wellspring of Internet availability so all PCs on the system are given Internet get to.

A remote switch isn't required for setting up a remote system. Practically any PC with a remote connector and a wired association with the Internet can be utilized as a passage. Next, the remote system must be given a name. This is generally alluded to as SSID. Every one of the PCs on a WLAN must have the equivalent SSID.

Every PC associated with the remote system should have a remote LAN card (likewise know as Wi-Fi connector) introduced. Wi-Fi connectors can be arranged after establishment of TCP/IP put together systems administration with respect to the individual PCs. On PCs utilizing Microsoft Windows working framework, connectors more often than not have their own realistic UI open from the taskbar after the remote systems administration equipment is introduced. This enables a client to enter the SSID and empower the WEP. For a WLAN to work precisely, every one of the connectors must utilize same parameter settings.

One can likewise settle on programmed remote arrangement that supports the IEEE-802.11 standard for remote systems. This limits the setup that is required to get to the remote system. When you empower programmed remote system setup on your PC, you can move crosswise over different systems without reconfiguring your system association settings. As you move starting with one spot then onto the next, programmed remote systems administration scans for a system that is accessible and informs you about the equivalent. You can choose the system that you need to interface with and the system design wizard refreshes your remote system connector to coordinate the setting of the passage of the new organize.

Regardless of whether you need to make a telephone call from your portable, get a message on your pager, or browse your email from a PDA, we have run over a remote information or voice organize. On the off chance that a client or an organization needs to make information compact, at that point Wireless systems administration is the appropriate response. A remote systems administration framework can maintain a strategic distance from the personal time, which might be caused in the wired system. A remote system additionally spares your time and endeavors in introducing the parcel of links.

Likewise, in the event that you have to move a customer machine in your office, you just need to move the PC with remote system card. Remote systems administration is valuable in the open spots, libraries, inns, schools, air terminals, railroad stations where one may discover remote access to the web. A downside in the remote web is that nature of administration (QOS) isn't ensured in the event that there is any obstruction, at that point the association might be dropped.

Remote Network Types

Remote Local Area Networks (WLANS)

WLANS permit clients in neighborhood, as in a college or a library to frame a system and addition remote access to the web. An impermanent system can be shaped by few clients without the need of passage; given that they don't have to get to the assets.

Remote Personal Area Networks (WPANS)

There are two current advances for remote individual system Bluetooth and Infra Red. These advances will permit the availability of individual gadgets inside a zone of 30 feet. Infra Red requires an immediate line and the range is less when contrasted with Bluetooth innovation.

Remote Metropolitan Area Networks (WMANS)

WMANS permit the availability of various systems in a metropolitan zone, for example, working in a city. The system availability is the option of copper or fiber cabling.

Remote Wide Area Networks (WWANS)

WWANS or Wireless Area Networks can be kept up over huge territories, for example, in various urban areas or between various nations, by means of different satellite frameworks or reception apparatus locales. The kinds of framework are called 2G frameworks.

The accompanying table demonstrates the range

those various kinds of remote system covers.

System Meter

Individual Area Network 0-10

Neighborhood 0-100

Wide Are Network 0-10000

Security in Wireless Networking

The accompanying various kinds of security strategies are accessible in the remote systems administration.

Kali Linux – Working with Nmap

The first step to working with nmap is to log into

the Kali Linux machine and if desired, start a graphical session. During the installation, the installer would have prompted the user for a 'root' user password which will be needed to login.

Once logged in to the Kali Linux machine, using the command 'startx' the Enlightenment Desktop Environment can be started – it is worth noting that nmap doesn't require a desktop environment to run.

Once logged into **Enlightenment**, a terminal window will need to be opened. By clicking on the desktop background, a menu will appear. Navigating to a terminal can be done as follows: **Applications** -> **System** -> **'Xterm'** or **'UXterm'** or **'Root Terminal'**.

CHAPTER SIX

How you can hack a wireless network

Wired Equivalent Privacy (WEP)

Wired Equivalent Privacy is planned to stop the obstruction of radio recurrence that is motioned by unapproved clients and this safety effort is most appropriate for the little arranges. There isn't key administration convention and each key is entered physically into the customers that is the reason this is exceptionally tedious regulatory undertaking. The WEP security strategy depends on the RC4 encryption calculation. In the WEP all the customer PCs and Access focuses are arranged with a similar encryption and decoding keys.

Administration Set Identifier (SSID)

Administration Set Identifier (SSID) acts a basic secret word by permitting WLAN system to be separated into various systems and each having a novel identifier. These identifiers are arranged in the different passages. To get to any of any systems, a PC is designed so that each is having a comparing SSID identifier for that arrange. In the event that the SSID coordinate between the two PCs or systems, at that point access is allowed to one another.

Media Access Control separating (MAC Access Control)

A rundown of the MAC locations of the customer PCs can be inputted into an Access point and just those PCs are allowed to give the penetrationto the system. At the point when a PC makes a solicitation, its MAC address is contrasted with the rundown of the MAC delivers to the Access point and dependent on this penetrationauthorization allowed to deny.

This is a decent security technique yet it is mostly associated with the little remote systems in light of the fact that there is progressively manual work is included of entering the MAC address into the Access point.

Bluetooth

Bluetooth is a basic sort of the remote systems administration that works in the computerized gadgets, similar to mobiles telephones, PCs, PDA, Laptops, advanced camera, MP3 players and other Bluetooth empowered gadgets to frame a little arrange. In the Bluetooth innovation eight gadgets can be associated with one another simultaneously. Bluetooth can likewise be found in the headsets, without hands units, remote consoles and mouse. Bluetooth innovation was created by Ericsson in 1994 and following four years in 1998 some real cell phone organizations, for example, Nokia, Ericsson, Intel and Toshiba shaped a gathering to advance this innovation.

Bluetooth innovation falls in the classification of individual territory organizing on the grounds that it works in the scope of 30 to 300 feet. Bluetooth utilizes the radio waves innovation, which isn't over the top expensive and has low control utilization. A wide range of organizations are expected to include the Bluetooth contribute their advanced gadgets. Bluetooth innovation is getting very notoriety as a result of its ease and compactness.

The Future of Wireless Networking

WLANS remote systems administration type is exceptionally well known in home systems administration and in excess of 20 percent homes with broadband web are utilizing WLANS and this number is expanding. In a general gauge overall hotspots have now arrived at more than 30,000 and will develop around 210,000 in the following couple of years. Most enormous inns officially offer Wi-Fi and the business explorers are eager to pay remote access. 802.11 is the following Wi-Fi speed standard is set to offer data transmission around 108Mbps is still a work in progress. With the speed of 70 Mbps and a range up to 30 miles, the 80216 standard, known as WiMAX is certain to get help.

WEP breaking

Breaking is the way toward misusing security shortcomings in remote systems and increasing unapproved get to. WEP breaking alludes to abuses on systems that utilization WEP to execute security controls. There are essentially two sorts of breaks to be specific;

• Passive splitting this sort of breaking has

no impact on the system traffic until the WEP security has been broken. It is hard to distinguish.

• Active splitting this sort of assault has an expanded burden impact on the system traffic. It is anything but difficult to recognize contrasted with aloof breaking. It is progressively successful contrasted with aloof breaking.

WEP Cracking Tools

• Aircrack–organize sniffer and WEP saltine. Can be downloaded from http://www.aircrack-ng.org/

• WEPCrack–this is an open source program for breaking 802.11 WEP mystery keys. It is an execution of the FMS assault. http://wepcrack.sourceforge.net/

• Kismet-this can incorporate identifier remote systems both obvious and covered up, sniffer parcels and identify interruptions. http://www.kismetwireless.net/

• WebDecrypt–this apparatus utilizes dynamic word reference assaults to break the WEP keys. It has its own key generator and executes parcel channels. http://wepdecrypt.sourceforge.net/

WPA Cracking

WPA utilizes a 256 pre-shared key or passphrase for confirmations. Short passphrases are defenseless against word reference assaults and different assaults that can be utilized to break passwords. The accompanying apparatuses can be utilized to split WPA keys.

• CowPatty–this instrument is utilized to split pre-shared keys (PSK) utilizing savage power assault. http://wirelessdefence.org/Contents/coWPAttyM ain.htm

• Cain and Abel–this instrument can be utilized to interpret catch documents from other sniffing projects, for example, Wireshark. The catch records may contain WEP or WPA-PSK encoded outlines. http://www.softpedia.com/get/Security/Decrypti ng-Decoding/Cain-and-Abel.shtml

General Attack types

• Sniffing–this includes capturing bundles as they are transmitted over a system. The caught information would then be able to be decoded utilizing instruments, for example, Cain and

Abel.

• Man in the Middle (MITM) Attack–this includes listening in on a system and catching touchy data.

• Denial of Service Attack–the principle plan of this assault is to deny genuine clients organize assets. FataJack can be utilized to play out this sort of assault. More on this in book

Splitting Wireless system WEP/WPA keys

It is conceivable to break the WEP/WPA keys used to access a remote system. Doing as such requires programming and equipment assets, and persistence. The accomplishment of such assaults can likewise rely upon how dynamic and inert the clients of the objective system are.

We will furnish you with essential data that can enable you to begin. Backtrack is a Linux-based security working framework. It is created over Ubuntu. Backtrack accompanies various security instruments. Backtrack can be utilized to accumulate data, evaluate vulnerabilities and perform abuses in addition to other things.

A portion of the mainstream apparatuses that backtrack has incorporates;

- Metasploit

- Wireshark

- Aircrack-ng

- NMap

- Ophcrack

Splitting remote system keys requires persistence and assets referenced previously. At any rate, you will require the accompanying devices

A remote system connector with the ability to infuse bundles (Hardware)

Step by step guide to hack wireless network using **Aircrack-ng**

STEP 1: PUT WI-FI ADAPTER IN MONITOR MODE WITH AIRMON-NG
- **airmon-ng start wlan0**

STEP 2: CAPTURE TRAFFIC WITH AIRODUMP-NG
- **airodump-ng mon0**

STEP 3: FOCUS AIRODUMP-NG ON ONE AP ON ONE CHANNEL
- **airodump-ng –bssid 08:86:30:74:22:76 -c 6 –write WPAcrack mon0**
- **08:86:30:74:22:76 is the BSSID of the AP**

- -c 6 is the channel the AP is operating on
- WPAcrack is the file you want to write to
- mon0 is the monitoring wireless adapter*

STEP 4: AIREPLAY-NG DEAUTH

- aireplay-ng –deauth 100 -a 08:86:30:74:22:76 mon0
- 100 is the number of de-authenticate frames you want to send
- 08:86:30:74:22:76 is the BSSID of the AP
- mon0 is the monitoring wireless adapter

STEP 5: CAPTURE THE HANDSHAKE

Notice in the top line to the far right, airodump-ng says "WPA handshake." The WPA handshake is the way it tells you were successful in grabbing the encrypted password! That is the first step to success!

STEP 6: LET'S AIRCRACK-NG THAT PASSWORD!

- aircrack-ng WPAcrack-01.cap -w /pentest/passwords/wordlists/darkc0de
- WPAcrack-01.cap is the name of the file we wrote to in the airodump-ng

command

- **/pentest/passwords/wordlist/darkc0de is the absolute path to your password file**

The most effective method to PROTECT YOUR WIRELESS NETWORK

Making a remote system at your home is a superb thought, it's extremely simple to do in addition to it empowers you to surf the net advantageously from anyplace at your house. The issue is that bunches of individuals are uninformed of the risk that is included when utilizing the home Wireless in a shaky way.

In the event that you need to ensure your WiFi so as to keep your neighbors from spending your data transmission, at that point sure that is a sound motivation to secure your WiFi, anyway it mustn't be your essential stress. The best issue with shaky WiFis happens when a programmer can interface with your WiFi, on the off chance that he prevails on doing that, at that point he can without much of a stretch read the data that is sent among you and the switch and uncover your usernames, passwords or everything else that is sent between your gadgets, paying little respect to whether you are utilizing SSL. This assault is known as "Man In The Middle" or MITM and it can without much of a stretch be performed by even a new kid on the block programmer rather rapidly. Verifying your Wireless will extraordinarily decrease the opportunity of this happening. Practically all programmers that attempt to get into WiFi's will rapidly quit any pretense of endeavoring to hack a safe remote system as there are endless unreliable systems out there which give an extensively less difficult objective.

The majority of the methodologies that will be clarified here necessitate that you sign in to your passage's UI and change a couple of its alternatives. On the off chance that you don't have a clue how to do that, at that point head toward your passage maker's site and search for the guide for your specific model. Attempt to discover data about how to access that switch's web interface.

1. Utilize a protected encryption

Utilizing a protected encryption is a basic strategy, this verifies you can just interface by utilizing a secret phrase. Picking this choices is commonly done from the security tab in the Wireless arrangement menu. You may for the most part pick from three or four choices: Disabled, WEP, WPA, WPA2. You'll need to pick WPA2 or WPA - and completely by no means pick impaired or WEP! WEP encryption is a very broken encryption calculation that can be broken in almost no time by a totally unpracticed programmer. On the off chance that your switch just underpins WEP encryption yet not WPA, at that point you ought to supplant that switch ASAP.

2. Use a solid encryption secret phrase

I'm sure you hear this expression a great deal "Utilize a solid secret key" and various individuals are contemplating internally that on WiFis it's not very significant, new streak - On WiFis it's critical to utilize solid passwords. Its a bit of cake for a programmer to utilize a program that sweeps the WiFi for many secret key mixes in minor minutes and split it. Use at any rate eight to ten characters and a blend of numbers, uncommon images and letters. Abstain from utilizing dates, names or telephones numbers - This is the absolute first thing programmers attempt.

3. Modify the SSID name

The SSID is the name of your remote system, it's that name you browse the rundown of adjacent systems when you attempt to join. It's suggested that you modify that name and not utilize the default name. Alter it to a name that doesn't totally uncover who is the person who claims this remote system, for example, your surname - this is particularly basic in case you're living in a thick populace zone for example a condo building.

4. Confine the Wifi's range

Limiting the transmit range will diminish the likelihood of somebody hoping to hack your system. In numerous homes the Wireless might be distinguished from outside of it and there's by and large no explanation behind this. Breaking point the transmission run, go outside your property and hope to see whether it could be found from that point. At the point when conceivable you may move your switch towards the focal point of the family to increase ideal inclusion without making vulnerable sides brought about by the confined Wireless system run.

5. Change the switch's interface security secret phrase

The switch's secret word is the secret phrase you have to type at whatever point signing in to the web interface. Actually in the event that the programmer can associate with the passageway's web interface, at that point it's as of now past the point of no return and the programmer has accessed the remote system as of now, however in any case, this is a decent insurance venture to take and it will constrain the control that the programmer has over your remote system. Change the secret word to a one that is hard to figure and is unique in relation to the one utilized for the encryption.

6. Check who is associated with the system

In the event that you presume that a gatecrasher is utilizing your WiFi, at that point most remote switches have an element that empowers you to check the IP and MAC locations of every gadget that is signed in to your passageway. You can look at that rundown and ensure that you know every one of the gadgets. This rundown is every now and again named dynamic DHCP rundown or something to that effect.

When you set in motion these pointers at that point you have an incredible possibility versus even the most persuaded programmers. Empowering these choices takes brief period and the security addition is extraordinarily significant. The majority of the tips are significant, anyway most fundamental one is encryption secret phrase, in the event that you don't embrace this tip then your system's security is totally broken.

CHAPTER SEVEN

The role of firewall

There exist some close to home firewalls that don't execute neither inbound nor outbound association assurance. In any case, these items likewise have bit drivers as a result of their subsequent capacity. The subsequent capacity is called sandbox. The most widely recognized strategies for the sandbox execution are SSDT snares and SSDT GDI snares. The driver of the firewall replaces some framework capacities with its very own code that confirms the privileges of calling application and either denies the activity or passes the execution to unique code. These strategies enables the firewall to control all the conceivable hazardous movement of uses, for example, endeavors to open documents, forms, library keys, alter firewall settings, consequently react to its inquiries and so on.

Framework administration

There are uncommon client mode procedures called framework administrations. These procedures have extraordinary capacities and conduct in the framework. They keep running under favored framework client instead of under regular client account. This reality enables administrations to run autonomously of client and they run additionally when no client is signed in. The job of administration in the individual firewall is to verify the correspondence between principle segments. The administration gets messages from the GUI and from the part driver and advances this messages to one another. For instance if the firewall is in the learning mode, the driver code in snared SSDT capacity might be not able choose whether to permit or deny the activity in light of the fact that there is no relating principle for the activity in the database. In such case it needs the client to

HACKING WITH KALI LINUX

choose. This requires to make an impression on GUI to demonstrate the exchange and to get the appropriate response from it. This correspondence is generally executed through the administration part. The administration of the firewall is here and there used to guarantee that the GUI is constantly accessible for the client.

Graphical UI

The graphical UI (GUI) is the client part of the firewall. It regularly actualizes a trayicon from which the organization of the firewall is accessible. Another significant capacity of the GUI is to approach client for the choice of activities when the firewall is in the learning mode.

Self-security

149

This is rule no. 1 for all security items, not just for individual firewalls. Regardless of the flawlessness of different highlights, if the firewall can't verify itself it is pointless. In the event that a pernicious action can turn off, impair or devastate the individual firewall it is proportional not to have any close to home firewall whatsoever. All pieces of the firewall must be ensured including its procedures, documents, library passages, drivers, administrations and other framework assets and books.

Confirmation of claim parts

The check of possess parts is near the previously mentioned Self-insurance. Firewalls are normally perplexing projects and they are regularly actualized in more than one module or part. In such case there are a couple of primary modules that are executed by the working framework. During the startup or in run these modules loads different modules of the firewall. We state that the modules are stacked powerfully. It is important to check the uprightness of all progressively stacked modules. This suggests the uprightness checker must be executed in one of the fundamental modules.

Inbound and outbound insurance

A decent close to home firewall offers both inbound and outbound security. The inbound assurance implies that parcels sent from the Internet or neighborhood to your PC are separated and just ports that you need to be open are available. This assurance is standard and is awesome and solid in practically all close to home firewalls. Then again is the outbound security which cause issues to all merchants these days. The outbound security implies that solitary applications that are permitted to can get to the Internet or neighborhood. This isn't as straightforward as it looks. Envision the circumstance that you need to peruse the Internet with your Internet program and that you don't need different applications to do as such. The issue here is that it isn't sufficient just to check which application needs to send the bundle to the Internet since present day working frameworks enables projects to impart. An application that isn't permitted to get to the Internet can begin the program and use it for the correspondence. Your own firewall needs to ensure each one of those advantaged applications against abusing by malware. It needs to confine the penetrationthem. Yet, this is as yet insufficient. The individual firewall needs to secure itself. Pernicious applications ought not have the option to turn it off or change its guidelines. This implies it likewise needs to ensure framework assets and so on. There are numerous issues in this despite everything we talk just around one component - the outbound assurance.

Procedure security

Each favored procedure must be secured against

a few hazardous activities. Right off the bat, no noxious application can end the procedure. Also, it must not be conceivable to alter its code or information. Thirdly, it must not be conceivable to execute any code in a setting of any favored procedure. This point additionally incorporates DLL infusion.

Document and segment insurance

The insurance of records is exceptionally near Process security. On the off chance that a malevolent code can supplant documents of special applications it is comparable to alter their code stream when they run. There are two different ways how to execute the assurance of documents. The principal way (dynamic security) is to avoid compose and erase access to records that have a place with special applications. Since this can be difficult to actualize numerous firewall coders pick the subsequent way - to check the respectability of modules (part security). For this situation the firewall enables vindictive code to harm or supplant records of favored applications. On the off chance that such application is going to run its modules are checked and the execution is ceased or answered to the client. The document security is likewise required for all framework records.

Driver insurance

Windows working frameworks trust its drivers. This imply each code that is controlled by the driver is trusted and along these lines it is permitted to execute even ensured processor's guidance and has potential access to all framework assets. This is the reason it is important to actualize a piece of security programming like individual firewall as a framework driver. Be that as it may, it is likewise why it is important to control stacking of new drivers and to secure existing drivers. Vindictive projects must not have the option to introduce drivers or alter effectively stacked drivers.

Administration security

Since a piece of the firewall is normally executed as a framework administration the security of framework administrations is additionally vital. Be that as it may, it isn't just the firewall segment that must be ensured. To introduce another administration is simple path for malware how to persevere in the framework since framework administrations can be set to run each framework begin. In addition, a malignant administration can be hazardous additionally in light of the fact that it runs regardless of whether no client is signed on. Creation, cancellation and control of framework administrations must be secured activities.

Library insurance

Windows library contains a great deal of significant framework data. Settings of framework segments can be changed utilizing the vault. An off base adjustment of some vault items can without much of a stretch reason framework to end up unsteady or incapable for sure. There are numerous vault keys and values that ought to be secured against adjustments of noxious applications.

Assurance of other framework assets

There are likewise extraordinary framework assets and items in Windows working frameworks. Some of them can be hazardous in the event that they are constrained by malware. One of these items is a notable segment 'DevicePhysicalMemory' which can be utilized to oversee the framework in the event that it isn't secured. The firewall must ensure those books that can be abused by malware.

Parent procedure control

We definitely realize that it is important to secure advantaged forms. Most likely the least demanding path how to actualize process security is to control opening of procedures and strings. Nonetheless, if the procedure insurance is actualize along these lines it is likewise imperative to execute Parent procedure control. Each procedure in the framework must be made by some different procedure - its parent. The parent is constantly given two handles when new it makes kid process. These are handle to the procedure book and handle to its principle string. The given procedure handle is opened with a full access and in this manner the parent procedure can control its kid totally. This is the reason the firewall must limit the execution of advantaged forms. Also, the parent procedure control ought to be actualized regardless of whether the firewall security configuration does not ensure forms by means of control of opening of procedures and strings. Some favored procedures can be abused to execute benefit activity on the off chance that they are kept running with explicit order line contentions. Numerous firewalls don't recognize the execution of favored and unprivileged forms. They limit the procedure creation when all is said in done with the end goal that solitary those applications that were chosen before can make tyke forms.

Control of naturally began projects

The firewall ought to ensure those spots in the working framework that can be utilized by malware to persevere in the framework after the reboot. In the event that we enable clients to run new obscure applications, at that point there is no possibility to ensure the framework against executing malevolent application. What's more, clients frequently download and introduce or run new applications. The firewall can limit activities of malignant applications with the end goal that they are not ready to harm the framework. Be that as it may, if the malware application perseveres in the framework it can harm it later when another security bug is found. This is the reason the firewall should control those applications that are run consequently for example after each framework begin or client logon.

Sniffing assurance

Spyware like keyloggers or parcel sniffers are risky applications since they are made to take the most delicate information clients can have - their passwords. Be that as it may, not just passwords are focuses of these applications. Individual data, individual correspondence or business archives are additionally touchy data that must be secured. The firewall needs to secure delicate information not just when they are finished in type of records yet in addition when they are made or being moved. Keyloggers can get each key stroke client makes and along these lines amass the entire data letter by letter. Parcel sniffers are trusting that the messages will be moved utilizing some system interface and they make duplicates of sent messages. There are numerous ways how to execute spyware projects to gather delicate information and every one of them must be secured by the firewall.

Move of information in a business framework frequently happens with the assistance of the advanced medium. In such a situation security of this information stays at the prime focal point of the considerable number of associations. Cryptography here assumes a critical job in keeping up the wellbeing of the moved information. Give us a chance to investigate the all through this procedure of center significance.

CHAPTER EIGHT

What are cryptography and digital signature

Cryptography is the strategy to conceal the data with the utilization of microdots, picture word combining, or with some different ways. In specialized field, it tends to be named as scrambling plain message into an encoded structure, for the most part called Ciphertext, of course to change over it into unscrambled configuration known as Cleartext. This procedure of encoding and unraveling is called cryptography and individuals rehearsing this field are known as cryptographers.

What are the Objectives of Cryptography?

Current cryptography pursues the beneath goals

1. Secrecy any individual who is out of the circle can't comprehend the data between the sender and collector.

2. Uprightness no adjustment is conceivable once the message is discharged.

3. Verification data, and sources in the cryptography framework are absolutely true. Both sender and beneficiary can recognize one another and starting point or goal of the data.

4. Non-disavowal none of the sender or collectors can venture back of the message at a later arrange.

5. Access control-just approved individuals can get to the classified information.

To satisfy the above targets the accompanying organizations of cryptography are polished

1. Symmetric cryptography-otherwise called mystery key cryptography, it is a strategy wherein both sender and collector share a similar mystery code and key for encryption and unscrambling. This strategy is helpful on the off chance that you are speaking with a predetermined number of individuals, in any case, it isn't much valuable for mass correspondence.

2. Hilter kilter cryptography-this is otherwise called open key cryptography in which, separate keys are utilized for encryption and decoding. This is valuable for key trade and computerized marks, for example, RSA, advanced mark calculation, open key cryptography standard and so forth.

3. Message-digest-in this, a hash capacity is utilized to for all time scramble the information. This is likewise called single direction encryption.

Cryptography ensures the system assets against change, devastation, and their unapproved use. They secure the system framework, IT resources, and the secret information. In the present situation, it has turned out to be very simple to modify or control the information and data. Burglary of private data is again a discomforting marvel.

Cryptographic systems have been being used since the season of the Sumerians (3500 BCE). Cryptography depends on mystery keys, which, as you'll review, are the contribution to the calculation that delivers the figure content. There are two fundamental sorts of cryptography: traditional cryptography and open key cryptography. In regular cryptography, a solitary key is utilized to perform both encryption and decoding. Since the keys are indistinguishable, they're alluded to as symmetric keys. Since just one key is utilized in customary cryptography, it's less secure. In the event that somebody other than the expected beneficiary finds the key, he can decode the first message. Another disadvantage to ordinary cryptography is that it's dangerous to disperse. On the off chance that somebody blocks the key on its way to the expected beneficiary, the security of the message is undermined. PGP Desktop additionally enables you to encode individual records and organizers, a part of your hard circle assigned as a virtual plate, or your whole hard circle.

In open key cryptography, two particular keys are utilized an open key to perform encryption and a private key to perform decoding. Since the keys are unique, they're alluded to as lopsided keys. This enables anybody to scramble a message yet just people with the relating private key to decode messages. To explain, we should take a gander at a model. On the off chance that Paul needs to make an impression on Sara, he utilizes Sara's open key to encode the message. At the point when Sara gets the message, she utilizes her private key to decode it. For whatever length of time that every individual in the message circle keeps his/her private key totally private, just the proposed beneficiary can unscramble the message. Open cryptography additionally defeats the dissemination issue in light of the fact that lone open keys should be sent over the shaky system; private keys are kept up locally.

Next, how about we direct our concentration toward a down to earth case of open key cryptography. In the accompanying segments, we'll utilize an example application, PGP Desktop, to tell you the best way to create an open/private key pair to verify both email and texts. We'll likewise tell you the best way to distribute your open key to the PGP Global Directory so others can send scrambled messages to you. At the point when your machine returns on the web, the PGP Setup Assistant dispatches consequently. This utility causes you complete an underlying arrangement, including producing another key pair and alternatively distributing your open key to the PGP Global Directory. Note that you should finish the PGP Setup Assistant errands preceding utilizing the essential application itself. Since PGP is introduced for all clients as a matter of course, you have to empower it for every window account exclusively. This implies you have to initially sign in with the proper Windows record, and afterward empower PGP for the dynamic record.

Computerized marks are viewed as the most significant improvement in open key cryptography. Sun Developer Network expresses, "A computerized mark is a series of bits that is processed from certain information (the information being "marked") and the private key of an element. The mark can be utilized to check that the information originated from the element and was not adjusted in travel" (The Java Tutorial, n.d.). Advanced marks ought to have the properties of creator check, confirmation of the date and time of the mark, verify the substance at the season of the mark, just as be irrefutable by an outsider so as to determine debates. In view of these properties, there are a few prerequisites for an advanced mark. The first of these prerequisites is that the mark must be a piece design that relies upon the message being agreed upon. The following necessity is announced so as to avoid phony and forswearing. It expresses that the mark must utilize some data that is exceptional to the sender. The third prerequisite is that it must be genuinely simple to create the computerized mark. Being moderately simple to perceive and confirm the computerized mark is another necessity. The fifth necessity expresses that it must be computationally infeasible to fashion a computerized mark, either by developing another message for a current advanced mark or by building a deceitful advanced mark for a given message. The last necessity is that it must be down to earth to store a duplicate of the advanced mark. Numerous methodologies for the execution of advanced marks have been proposed, and they fall into the direct and mediated computerized mark draws near

(Stallings, 2003).

The direct advanced mark includes just correspondence between the source and goal parties, and the parleyed computerized mark plans incorporate the utilization of a mediator. The direct advanced mark is made by scrambling the whole message or a hash code of the message with the sender's private key. Further classification can be given by encoding the message completely and including mark utilizing either the recipient's open key or a mystery key shared between the sender and beneficiary. One shortcoming in the immediate mark plan is that a sender can later deny having communicated something specific. Another shortcoming is the danger of a private key being stole and communicating something specific utilizing the mark. The two shortcomings are the essential explanation behind the refereed computerized mark conspire. In mediated plan, a sender's message should initially experience a mediator that runs a progression of tests to check the source and substance before it is sent to the collector. Since the judge assumes such a critical job, the sender and recipient must have a lot of trust in this mediator. This trust in the referee guarantees the sender that nobody can fashion his mark and guarantees the collector that the sender can't abandon his mark (Stallings, 2003).

This book isn't about the historical backdrop of Unix; in any case, Unix is such a mind boggling issue, that it merits few words in this regard: BSD group of Unix frameworks depends on the source code of genuine Unix created in Bell Labs, which was later bought by the University of California. In this manner, the name of the group of Unix frameworks called BSD is gotten from "Berkeley Software Distribution". The contemporary BSD frameworks remain on the source code that was discharged in the start of 1990's (Net/2 Lite and 386/BSD discharge).

Nobody individual or any element claims BSD. Energetic designers make it and huge numbers of its parts are publicly released.

BSD is behind the way of thinking of TCP/IP organizing and the Internet thereof; it is a created Unix framework with cutting edge highlights. With the exception of exclusive BSD/OS, the improvement of which was stopped, there are presently four BSD frameworks accessible: FreeBSD, NetBSD, OpenBSD and Mac OS X, which is gotten from FreeBSD. There are likewise different forks of these, similar to PC-BSD - a FreeBSD clone, or MirOS, an OpenBSD clone. The expectation of such forks is to incorporate different qualities missing in the above BSD frameworks, on which these (forks), regardless of how well they are planned, just emphatically depend. PC-BSD, for instance, has more graphical highlights than FreeBSD, however there are no significant contrasts between these two. PC-BSD can't inhale without FreeBSD; FreeBSD or OpenBSD are autonomous of each other.

What is Linux?

Yet clients like to utilize the expression "Linux" for any Linux distro including its bundles (Red Hat Linux, Mandrake Linux, and so forth.), for IT experts Linux is just the portion. Linux began in 1991, when its creator, Linus Torvals, started his work on a free substitution of Minix. Designers of many Linux framework utilities utilized the source code from BSD, as both these frameworks began parallelly in about a similar time (1992-1993) as Open Source.

Today, there are a couple, if relatively few engineers of their own portions/working frameworks (FreeDOS, Agnix, ReactOS, Inferno, and so forth.), however these folks just missed the correct train in the correct hour. They didn't lose anything aside from the way that they might be far superior developers, yet without the general conclusion recognizing this on the loose. Linus constructed his acclaim likewise from work of numerous designers and he got onto in the correct time. Linus merits a credit as a product thought arrangement creator and he helped particularly in this regard.

(Open)BSD versus Linux

It is regularly hard to state what is better in the event that you look at two things without in regards to the reason for their utilization. Portable Internet may show up better for somebody who voyages regularly, however for individuals working at home such portability isn't important. In this view, it is an inept inquiry when somebody pose: "What is better, a versatile or static Internet?" everything depends...

In the event that you think about Linux and OpenBSD in their work area condition highlights, Linux offers a bigger number of utilizations than OpenBSD; yet in a server arrangement BSD frameworks are known to be powerful, progressively steady and secure, and without such a significant number of patches merchants discharge not long after their new form of Linux crawled to light.

BSD frameworks depend on genuine Unix source code in opposition to Linux, which was created sans preparation (piece).

Contrasts among BSD and Linux

1) BSD permit permits clients/organizations to alter a program's source code and not to discharge changes to general society. As it were, BSD licenses permit business use and consolidation of a code into exclusive business items. This is the manner by which Microsoft consolidated BSD organizing into their items and how Mac OS X wins cash through muscles of FreeBSD.

Linux utilizes GPL permit for more often than not (applications in Linux can likewise have a BSD permit - or any permit; it is up to engineers how they choose). With a GPL-authorized program anyone can change the source code, however the person MUST impart it to the Open Source people group to ensure that everyone will profit by such a change.

2) BSD has the supposed "center framework" (without bundles). The center framework comprises of fundamental utilities (like ssh, fdisk, different directions like chmod or sysctl, manual pages, and so on.) and anything past this is carefully observed as an extra. Linux (not just the piece, obviously) is normally bundled as the entire framework where this distinction isn't seen.

3) On BSD frameworks, all extra bundles are carefully introduced into the/usr/neighborhood catalog: archives to client/nearby/share/docs/application_name; subjects and different things to/usr/nearby/share/application_name; parallels to/usr/nearby/canister/application_name. By application_name we mean a program's name, so

in the event that you introduce IceWM, for instance, its twofold will be here:/usr/neighborhood/container/icewm. With Linux, then again, all applications get generally introduced into the/usr/receptacle registry.

4) BSD frameworks utilize the arrangement of "ports", which are fingerprints of utilizations in the/usr/ports catalog, where a client may "disc" and execute a make order, which will download, by means of a mandate contained in such a unique mark's code, the application's source and the framework will assemble it too. "Ports" are really add-on bundles for BSD frameworks and they are likewise bundled in bundles store of a solid BSD framework. They can be introduced as pairs, as well, with utilization of the "pkg_add" either legitimately from the Internet or locally. In any case, "ports" have that favorable position that if a creator of any bundle makes another adaptation, a client can promptly get its freshest/refreshed variant. Bundles discharged for a specific BSD rendition (like OpenBSD 4.1) are not refreshed and clients need to sit tight for

another BSD discharge (like OpenBSD 4.2).

5) BSD frameworks have additionally their steady form. With FreeBSD, for instance, you have a FreeBSD-Release (an adaptation that can be utilized typically), FreeBSD-Stable (framework all the more significantly inspected for bugs and security openings), and an improvement rendition - Current, which isn't steady and not suggested for an ordinary use. Some Linux disseminations began to mirror this way of thinking, however with BSD frameworks along these lines of making dispersions has turned into a standard.

6) obviously, the piece is totally unique.

7) BSD has FFS record framework; it is the main document framework on BSD's in opposition to Linux, where you can utilize many document frameworks like ext2, ext3, ReiserFS, XFS, and so

forth.

8) BSD frameworks separate their segments inside. This implies subsequent to introducing a BSD framework to a hard circle, programs like fdisk, Partition Magic, Norton Ghost and numerous others won't see this interior division of a BSD (FFS) plate; along these lines, repartitioning of a plate isn't such a torment when managers require a thorough apportioning (for/home,/tmp,/var,/and so on indexes). As an outcome, the naming show additionally varies a little: a plate -/dev/ad0s3b in FreeBSD demonstrates that you manage "cut" 3 ("s3"), which is what might be compared to Linux/dev/hda3; the inside "parcel" has the name of a letter: "a", "b", "e", and so on ("b" is a swap segment). BSD frameworks likewise utilize diverse naming shows for gadgets (plates, and so on.).

9) Unless you make a decent portion hack, BSD frameworks must be introduced into the

essential segment. This isn't the standard with Linux. Be that as it may, as BSD frameworks offer the previously mentioned inward division of allotments, this isn't any agony. PC design for circles (IDE) pursues the standard that you can have just four essential parcels. We will represent this on Linux:/dev/hda1 (note: first segment on ace plate on first IDE channel),/dev/hda2 (second segment),/dev/hda3 (third parcel),/dev/hda4 (fourth segment). PC design permits formation of the alleged coherent plate on a physical circle (/dev/hda5,/dev/hda6, and so forth.). You can have the same number of consistent circles/segments as you wish and you can likewise introduce Linux into these "sensible plates". Then again, introducing a BSD OS into such a "coherent segment" isn't regularly conceivable.

10) System arrangement is manual for more often than not, yet different clones like PC-BSD break this show. The manual methodology is a generally excellent thing, as chairmen have everything leveled out without being pushed to

sit around idly in a maze of enlarged design menus. A decent correlation is to envision an auto technician fixing the's motor secured by a thick cover. To give you even a little better model - you will scarcely discover a Linux distro that does not have a default X startup (graphical condition). Obviously, you can turn off the X condition during the establishment arrangement, however in the event that you keep overlooking like me and neglect to turn this off, or you experience issues to discover it in the menu some place, you understand that most Linux merchants do for sure force on us just one methodology - to put our fingers first on the thick cover, at that point on the motor. On the off chance that you are a decent manager, you don't normally confide in sellers who program you how to utilize Linux - you are the supervisor and you should have your own opportunity. Nonetheless, much of the time you lose couple of hours rather by deactivating different administrations, which are, tragically, not in any case vital however quite often enacted as a matter of course. Linux is commended both for being a decent work area and server, yet chairmen of a decent server needn't bother with X. The more programming is put away on your hard circle, the greater security issues you will confront, in light of the fact that it is difficult to review each bundle in each unfathomable circumstance. Great and secure frameworks are in every case tight, light and straightforward.

11) All BSD frameworks have a Linux copying support. Running BSD parallels on Linux is somewhat harder.

12) BSD frameworks have less help from driver merchants, consequently they linger behind in this view (they are not more awful, however numerous sellers bolster just Microsoft and Linux). With a BSD framework you should cautiously inquire about the Internet for upheld items/chipsets before acquiring any equipment.

13) BSD frameworks don't utilize the Unix

System V "runlevel contents" (instatement startup

The issue of replay assaults is a principle concern when managing common confirmation when the two gatherings are affirming the other's personality and trading session keys. The essential issues with common verification lies in the key trade: secrecy and courses of events. Timetables are defenseless to replay assaults that upset activities by giving gatherings messages that seem veritable yet are definitely not. One sort of replay assault is smother answer assault that can happen in the Denning convention. The Denning convention utilizes a timestamps to expand security. The issue here rotates around the dependence on tickers that are synchronized all through the system. It is expressed, "...that the dispersed timekeepers can end up unsynchronized because of treachery on or blames in the tickers or the synchronization system" (Stallings, 2003 p. 387). Li Gong states, "...the beneficiary stays defenseless against tolerating the message as a present one, even after the sender has distinguished its clock blunder and resynchronized the clock, except if the postdated message has in the interim been by one way or another refuted," which is impossible. On the off chance that the clock of the sender is in front of the recipients and the message is blocked, the adversary can replay the message when the timestamp ends up current. This sort of assault is known as stifle replay assault.

So as to address the worry of smother replay assault, an improved convention was exhibited. Here are the definite advances.

CHAPTER NINE

What are VPN, TOR and Proxy chains and how to use them for security

A VPN, or Virtual Private Network, enables you to make a protected association with another system over the Internet. VPNs can be utilized to get to district confined sites, shield your perusing movement from prying eyes on open Wi-Fi, and that's only the tip of the iceberg.

Nowadays VPNs are extremely well known, yet not for the reasons they were initially made. They initially were only an approach to interface business organizes together safely over the web or enable you to get to a business arrange from home.

VPNs basically forward the entirety of your

system traffic to the system, which is the place the advantages – like getting to neighborhood organize assets remotely and bypassing Internet control – all originate from. Most working frameworks have incorporated VPN support.

Tor is short for The Onion Router (accordingly the logo) and was at first an overall system of servers created with the U.S. Naval force that empowered individuals to peruse the web secretly. Presently, it's a non-benefit association whose principle intention is the innovative work of online security devices.

The Tor system camouflages your character by moving your traffic crosswise over various Tor servers, and scrambling that traffic so it isn't followed back to you. Any individual who attempts would see traffic originating from arbitrary hubs on the Tor organize, as opposed to your PC.

Various needs and distinctive danger models lead to misconception between individuals. Suppose you need to leave the most mysterious remark conceivable on some informal community. What do you requirement for it? VPN? Tor? A SSH burrow? Indeed, it's sufficient to purchase any SIM card and an utilized telephone at a closest shop, at that point go at an impressive good ways from where you live, embed one into another, post your message, and sink the telephone. You have achieved your main goal at 100%.

Be that as it may, imagine a scenario where you would prefer not to simply leave a one-time remark or conceal your IP address from some site. Consider the possibility that you need such a propelled degree of secrecy that will make up the most multifaceted riddle with no space for any hack on any level. And furthermore hide the very truth of utilizing obscurity devices in transit? This is what I'm going to discuss in this piece.

The ideal namelessness is generally a fantasy, such as everything immaculate. Be that as it may, it doesn't mean you can't approach it quite close. Regardless of whether you're being recognized by framework fingertips and different methods, you can even now remain undistinguishable from the mass of general Web clients. In this book I will disclose how to accomplish this.

This isn't an invitation to take action, and the creator in no way, shape or form requires any illicit activities or infringement of any laws of any states. Think of it as only a dream about "in the event that I were a government agent."

Fundamental security level

The fundamental degree of security and namelessness looks generally along these lines: customer → VPN/TOR/SSH burrow → target.

As a matter of fact, this is only a somewhat further developed rendition of an intermediary which permits to substitute your IP. You won't accomplish any genuine or quality namelessness along these lines. Only one inaccurate or default setting in famous WebRTC, and your genuine IP is uncovered. This sort of security is likewise helpless against hub trading off, fingerprints, and even basic log examination with your supplier and server farm.

Coincidentally, there is a typical assessment that a private VPN is superior to anything an open one since the client is sure about his framework arrangement. Consider for a minute that somebody knows your outside IP. Consequently, he realizes your server farm as well. Henceforth, the server farm knows the server this IP has a place with. What's more, presently simply envision that it is so hard to figure out which real IP associated with the server. Imagine a scenario in which you are the just a single customer there.

What's more, on the off chance that they are various, for instance 100, it's getting a lot harder.

What's more, this isn't referencing that not many individuals will try scrambling their circles and shielding them from physical expulsion, so they will scarcely see that their servers are rebooted with init level 1 and exchanging on VPN signs on a reason of "minor specialized challenges in the server farm." Furthermore, there's no need even in things like these, in light of the fact that all your inbound and outbound server locations are as of now known.

Talking about Tor, its utilization itself can raise doubts. Besides, the outbound hubs are just around 1000, a significant number of them are blocklisted, and they are no-no for some locales. For instance, Cloudfare highlights a capacity to empower or impair Tor associations by methods for a firewall. Use T1 as the nation. In addition, Tor is much more slow than VPN (right now the Tor system speed is under 10 Mbit/s and regularly 1-3 Mbit/s).

Outline: If all you need is to abstain from demonstrating your international ID to everybody, sidestep basic site squares, have a quick association, and course all the traffic through another hub, pick VPN, and it should be a paid administration. For a similar cash, you'll get many nations and hundreds and even a huge number of outbound IPs as opposed to a VPS with a solitary nation that you'll have to agonizingly set up.

For this situation it's little sense to utilize Tor, however at times Tor will be an average arrangement, particularly on the off chance that you have an additional layer of security like VPN or a SSH burrow. Progressively about this further down.

Medium insurance level

A medium insurance level resembles a propelled form of the fundamental one: customer → VPN → Tor and varieties. This is an ideal working apparatus for any individual who fears IP mocking. This is an instance of cooperative energy when one innovation reinforces the other. Be that as it may, don't be mixed up however. While it's extremely hard to acquire your real address, you are as yet helpless against every one of the assaults depicted previously. Your frail chain is your working environment - your work PC.

High assurance level

Customer → VPN → Remote work environment (by means of RDP/VNC) → VPN.

Your work PC ought not be yours, however a remote machine with, state, Windows 8, Firefox, several modules like Flash, couple of codecs, and no one of a kind text styles and different modules. An exhausting and plain machine undistinguishable for millions out there. If there should be an occurrence of any hole or trading off, despite everything you'll be secured by another VPN.

It was accepted already that Tor/VPN/SSH/Socks permitted an abnormal state of obscurity, however today I would prescribe adding a remote working environment to this arrangement.

Great

Customer → Double VPN (in various server farms, however near one another) → Remote working environment + Virtual machine → VPN.

The proposed plan comprises of an essential VPN association and an auxiliary VPN association (on the off chance that if the first VPN is undermined because of some break). It serves to conceal traffic from the ISP with the objective to cover your genuine ISP address in the server farm with a remote work environment. Next goes a virtual machine introduced on the server. I guess you comprehend why a virtual machine is so essential - to move back to the most standard and worn-out framework with a standard arrangement of modules after each download. Also, this ought to be done on a remote work environment as opposed to a nearby one, in light of the fact that the individuals who utilized a virtual machine locally alongside TripleVPN once opened IP checking webpage and got very shocked seeing their genuine and genuine IP address in the "WebRTC" field. I don't have the foggiest idea and would prefer not to realize what programming some designer will grow tomorrow and introduce in your program without your worry. So simply don't consider it and don't store anything locally. Kevin Mitnick knew it 30 years back.

We have tried this arrangement, slacks are huge regardless of whether you design everything appropriately as far as topography. Be that as it may, these slacks are average. We accept that the client won't put the servers on various mainlands. For instance, in the event that you are physically situated in New York, place your first VPN additionally in New York, the second one in Mexico and so on., your remote working environment in Canada, and the last VPN, state, in Venezuela. Try not to put various servers in the Euro zone since those legislatures coordinate firmly, yet then again, don't spread them excessively a long way from one another. Neighboring nations that abhor each other would be the best answer for your chain;)

You could likewise include the programmed visiting of sites in foundation from your real machine along these lines copying Web surfing. By this you dissipate doubts that you utilize some secrecy devices on the grounds that your traffic consistently goes to just a single IP address and through one port. You could include Whonix/Tails and go online through an open Wi-Fi in a bistro, however simply in the wake of changing your system connector settings which could likewise prompt your deanonymization. You could even change your looks all together not to be recognized outwardly in the equivalent bistro. You can be recognized by various methods beginning from your directions in a photograph caught by your telephone to your composition style. Simply recall that.

Then again, most of individuals are impeccably fit with an anonymizer, yet even our anonymizer after the entirety of our endeavors to make it helpful is as yet deficient regarding surfing background. Indeed, a standard VPN is an ordinary and legitimate answer for bypassing basic squares with a conventional speed. Need greater namelessness and prepared to forfeit some speed? Add Tor to the blend. Need some more? Do as previously mentioned.

Fingerprints, similar to endeavors to identify VPN use, are hard to sidestep because of the season of sending bundles from the client to the site and from the site to the client's IP address (without considering blocking just explicit inbound solicitations). You can swindle a couple of checks, yet you can't make sure that another "bad dream" won't show up medium-term. This is the reason you need a remote work environment so severely, just as a clean virtual machine. So it's the best guidance you can get right now. The expense of such an answer begins from just $40 every month. In any case, observe you should pay with Bitcoin as it were.

What's more, a little afterword. The primary and most significant factor of your achievement in accomplishing genuine obscurity is isolating individual and mystery information. Every one of the passages and mind boggling plans will be totally pointless in the event that you sign in, for example, your own Google account.

Be unknown!

https://whoer.net is an administration planned for checking the data your PC

CHAPTER TEN

How to spoof addresses

Macintosh address ridiculing is a system for incidentally changing your Media Access Control (MAC) address on a system gadget. A MAC Address is an interesting and hardcoded address customized into system gadgets which can't be changed forever. The MAC address is in the second OSI layer and ought to be viewed as the physical location of your interface. Macchanger is an instrument that is incorporated with any rendition of Kali Linux including the 2016 moving release and can change the MAC address to any ideal location until the following reboot. In this instructional exercise we will parody the MAC address of our remote connector with an irregular MAC address created by Macchanger on Kali Linux.

◎   First we have to bring down the system connector so as to change the MAC address. This should be possible utilizing the accompanying direction: The ifconfig instrument will be supplanted by iproute2. Utilize the accompanying direction to bring down wlan1 with iproute2:

- ➤ Replace wlan1 with your own system interface.

- ➤ Now utilize the accompanying direction to change your MAC address to another irregular MAC Address:

- ➤ As appeared on the screen capture, Macchanger will demonstrate to you the perpetual, current and changed MAC address. The lasting MAC Address will be reestablished to your system connector after a reboot or you can reset your system connectors MAC address physically. Utilize the accompanying direction to reestablish the perpetual MAC address to your system connector physically:

➢ You can likewise parody a specific MAC address utilizing the accompanying direction: ifconfig wlan1 up

➢ Or utilize the accompanying iproute2 direction to bring the wlan1 gadget back up: ip connection set wlan1 up

A developing position of Internet hooligans are currently utilizing new deceives called "phishing" and "ridiculing" to take your personality. Sham messages that endeavor to fool clients into giving out close to home data are the most sizzling new trick on the Internet.

"Parodying" or "phishing" cheats endeavor to cause web clients to accept that they are getting email from a particular, confided in source, or that they are safely associated with a believed site, when that is not the situation by any stretch of the imagination, a long way from it. Mocking is commonly utilized as a way to persuade people to reveal individual or money related data which empowers the culprits to submit charge card/bank extortion or different types of wholesale fraud.

> ➤ In "email ridiculing" the header of an email seems to start from somebody or some place other than the genuine source. Spam merchants frequently use email mocking trying to get their beneficiaries to open the message and perhaps even react to their sales.

"IP ridiculing" is a system used to increase unapproved access to PCs. In this example the deceitful interloper makes an impression on a PC with an IP address showing that the message is originating from a confided in source.

"Connection change" includes the modifying of

an arrival web address of a page that is messaged to a shopper so as to divert the beneficiary to a programmer's website as opposed to the authentic webpage. This is cultivated by including the programmer's IP address before the genuine location in an email which has a solicitation returning to the first site. On the off chance that an individual accidentally gets a satirize email and continues to "click here to refresh" account data, for instance, and is diverted to a site that looks precisely like a business site, for example, eBay or PayPal, there is a decent shot that the individual will finish in submitting individual as well as credit data. Furthermore, that is actually what the programmer is relying on.

The most effective method to Protect Yourself

· If you have to refresh your data on the web, utilize a similar strategy you've utilized previously, or open another program window and type in the site address of the genuine organization's page.

· If a site's location is new, it's likely not real. Just utilize the location that you've utilized previously, or even better, begin at the typical landing page.

· Most organizations expect you to sign in to a protected site. Search for the lock at the base of your program and "https" before the site address.

· If you experience a spontaneous email that demands, either straightforwardly or through a site, for individual budgetary or personality data, for example, Social Security number, passwords, or different identifiers, practice outrageous alert.

· Take note of the header address on the site. Most real locales will have a generally short web address that typically delineates the business name pursued by ".com," or potentially ".organization." Spoof destinations are bound to have an exorbitantly long solid of characters in the header, with the real business name some place in the string, or perhaps not in the least.

· If you have any questions about an email or site, contact the real organization legitimately. Make a duplicate of the flawed site's URL address, send it to the genuine business and inquire as to whether the solicitation is authenti

How computerize undertakings

For the individuals who don't have the foggiest idea how full scale programming computerizes undertakings, or whether they even have large scale programming, the basic answer is that you perused this book and after that you have a total comprehension of how full scale programming robotizing assignments.

Keeping an eye on similar locales, recollecting passwords, submitting to look through architects, just as testing sites again and again are the dreary undertakings for each internet browser ordinary. What's more, filling structures, running projects at a specific time, messing around, just as planning errands consistently are dull redundancy. Your undertaking can be any of those monotonous assignments. On the off chance that at least one of these assignments are happening each day, mechanizing these monotonous undertakings will assist you with saving your valuable time and to improve efficiency.

There are two fundamental approaches to computerize dull assignments - record keystroke and mouse exercises or alter content physically with full scale programming. Both of the ways can be spared as a full scale and later it would be replayed by utilizing any of these strategies -

hotkey, scheduler and trigger. Clearly, attempted these errands by chronicle keystroke and mouse exercises is a basic way. Nonetheless, the way can not finish those unpredictable assignments except if the undertakings are finished just by utilizing keystroke and mouse exercises, for example, clicking catches on a window. So for those mind boggling errands, there is an a lot simpler and faster way - alter content physically.

To start utilizing along these lines, you should comprehend what content manager is in large scale programming. Large scale content manager is a device for altering full scale activities. Albeit a large scale can be made by account, in any case, the chronicle just catches the mouse and the console exercises. In this manner, for getting other complex activities, for example, sitting tight for a window centered, you can utilize content editorial manager worked in large scale programming to alter these activities and computerize to execute them later.

By utilizing thusly, you can computerize any arrangement of undertakings on your PC, running from just individual errands, to complex business assignments and significantly more. Simultaneously, you can utilize large scale programming to effectively make the errands: browsing email, moving or support up documents, sending email, and progressively complex computerization, including restrictive IF/ELSE explanations, circles, factors and other propelled alternatives.

Presently, you have realized how large scale programming robotizes assignments. In the event that you have no one, you have to either download a free or preliminary duplicate from the web, or buy a duplicate of your picked programming.

CHAPTER ELEVEN

Bash scripting and python scripting

What is bash Scripting?

A shell script is basically a text file that contains containing a string of commands in sequence. When the script is run, it executes all the commands that are in the file. The "shell" in the phrase refers to the command-line user interface that is used to communicate with the Linux kernel. There are a few different shells currently in use, with the most common ones being the C shell or csh, the Korn shell or ksh, the Bourne shell or sh, and the Bourne-Again shell or bash.

There are a number of scenarios that will require you to script with the shell. You may for instance have to support existing scripts, or you may wish to automate the system setup procedure before installing Oracle. In this scenario, you may use a script to determine the state of the operating system and any system requirements that you will have to meet before the software can be installed.

Linux

The most commonly used shell under Linux is called "Bash". This name is derived from "Bourne Again Shell". Although there are many other types of shells available for Linux, most experts recommend that you stick to the Bash shell, since this will increase the portability of your scripts between different systems and operating systems.

UNIX

Under UNIX, the shell allows a programmer to string together and execute a number of UNIX commands without having to compile them first. This makes it a lot faster to get a script running. In addition, shell scripting under UNIX makes it easier for other programmers to read and understand your code. Such shell scripts are also usually easily portable across the entire UNIX world, as long as they conform to a set standard.

Scripting for Windows

The Windows operating system conveniently includes a basic command structure that can be used to create scripts that will essentially streamline various administrative tasks. Some of the more common scripting languages under the Windows platform are Windows shell scripting, Visual Basic Scripting or VBS, and JScript. Shell scripting on the Windows platform is commonly used to produce logon scripts, which are in turn used to configure the Windows environment for specific uses when they log on. Marketing personnel for instance may use such scripts to automatically map network drives to the marketing network folder, and so on.

Despite what assembly code and C coders might tell us, high-level languages do have their place in every programmer's toolbox, and some of them are much more than a computer-science curiosity. Out of the many high-level languages we can choose from today, Python seems to be the most interesting for those who want to learn something new and do real work at the same time. Its no-nonsense implementation of object-oriented programming and its clean and easy-to-understand syntax make it a language that is fun to learn and use, which is not something we can say about most other languages.

In Python Training, you will learn how to write applications that use command-line options, read and write to pipes, access environment variables, handle interrupts, read from and write to files, create temporary files and write to system logs. In other words, you will find recipes for writing real applications instead of the old boring Hello, World! stuff.

Getting Started

To begin, if you have not installed the Python interpreter on your system, now is the time. To make that step easier, install the latest Python distribution using packages compatible with your Linux distribution. rpm, deb and tgz are also available on your Linux CD-ROM or on-line. If you follow standard installation procedures, you should not have any problems.

I also recommend that you have the Python Library Reference handy; you might want it when the explanations given here do not meet your needs. You can find it in the same places as the Python Tutorial.

Creating scripts can be done using your favorite text editor as long as it saves text in plain ASCII format and does not automatically insert line breaks when the line is longer than the width of the editor's window.

Always begin your scripts with either

#! /usr/local/bin/python

or

#! /usr/bin/python

If the access path to the python binary on your system is different, change that line, leaving the first two characters (#!) intact. Be sure this line is truly the first line in your script, not just the first non-blank line-it will save you a lot of frustration.

Use chmod to set the file permissions on your

script to make it executable. If the script is for you alone, type chmod 0700 scriptfilename.py; if you want to share it with others in your group but not let them edit it, use 0750 as the chmod value; if you want to give access to everyone else, use the value 0755. For help with the chmod command, type man chmod.

Reading Command-Line Options and Arguments

Command-line options and arguments come in handy when we want to tell our scripts how to behave or pass some arguments (file names, directory names, user names, etc.) to them. All programs can read these options and arguments if they want, and your Python scripts are no different.

Bash script can be utilized for different purposes, for example, executing a shell order, running various directions together, tweaking managerial errands, performing task robotization and so on. So information of slam programming nuts and bolts is significant for each Linux client. This section will assist you with getting the fundamental thought on slam programming. A large portion of the regular activities of slam scripting are clarified with extremely basic models here.

Bash script can be utilized for different purposes, for example, executing a shell direction, running various directions together, modifying managerial errands, performing task robotization and so on. So learning of slam programming nuts and bolts is significant for each Linux client. This part will assist you with getting the essential thought on slam programming.

A typical example of bash scripting is sh-bang #!/bin/bash -e and an example of python scripting is magic 8-ball and port scanner in phyth

Penetration test with Metasploit

In the event that you are new to the universe of working framework programming and shell scripting, huge numbers of the terms and ideas will probably stable Greek to you. Except if you are Greek obviously, in which case it would seem like Chinese! The truth is that shell scripting can be confounding, despite the fact that it gets more clear with time. This book covers the very nuts and bolts of shell scripting and will rapidly get you making a course for edification.

What is slam Scripting?

A shell content is fundamentally a content record that contains containing a series of directions in arrangement. At the point when the content is run, it executes every one of the directions that are in the document. The "shell" in the expression alludes to the direction line UI that is utilized to speak with the Linux bit. There are a couple of various shells at present being used, with the most well-known ones being the C shell or csh, the Korn shell or ksh, the Bourne shell or sh, and the Bourne-Again shell or slam.

There are various situations that will expect you to content with the shell. You may for example need to help existing contents, or you may wish to robotize the framework arrangement system before introducing Oracle. In this situation, you may utilize a content to decide the condition of the working framework and any framework prerequisites that you should meet before the product can be introduced.

Linux

The most regularly utilized shell under Linux is classified "Slam". This name is gotten from "Bourne Again Shell". In spite of the fact that there are numerous different kinds of shells accessible for Linux, most specialists prescribe that you adhere to the Bash shell, since this will expand the versatility of your contents between various frameworks and working frameworks.

UNIX

Under UNIX, the shell enables a software engineer to string together and execute various UNIX directions without gathering them first. This makes it significantly quicker to get a content running. What's more, shell scripting under UNIX makes it simpler for different developers to peruse and comprehend your code. Such shell contents are additionally for the most part effectively convenient over the whole UNIX world, as long as they adjust to a set standard.

Scripting for Windows

The Windows working framework helpfully incorporates a fundamental direction structure that can be utilized to make contents that will basically streamline different managerial errands. A portion of the more typical scripting dialects under the Windows stage are Windows shell scripting, Visual Basic Scripting or VBS, and JScript. Shell scripting on the Windows stage is usually used to deliver logon contents, which are thusly used to arrange the Windows condition for explicit uses when they sign on. Showcasing faculty for example may utilize such contents to consequently guide system drives to the promoting system envelope, etc.

Notwithstanding what get together code and C coders may let us know, abnormal state dialects do have their place in each software engineer's tool compartment, and some of them are substantially more than a software engineering interest. Out of some abnormal state dialects we can browse today, Python is by all accounts the most fascinating for the individuals who need to discover some new information and do genuine work simultaneously. Its straightforward usage of item situated programming and its perfect and straightforward punctuation make it a language that is enjoyable to learn and utilize, which isn't something we can say about most different dialects.

Beginning

To start, on the off chance that you have not introduced the Python translator on your framework, this is the ideal opportunity. To make that progression simpler, introduce the most recent Python appropriation utilizing bundles perfect with your Linux conveyance. rpm, deb and tgz are additionally accessible on your Linux CD-ROM or on-line. On the off chance that you pursue standard establishment systems, you ought not have any issues.

I likewise prescribe that you have the Python Library Reference helpful; you may need it when the clarifications given here don't address your issues. You can discover it in indistinguishable spots from the Python Tutorial.

Making contents should be possible utilizing your preferred word processor as long as it spares message in plain ASCII design and does not consequently embed line breaks when the line is longer than the width of the manager's window.

Continuously start your contents with either

#! /usr/neighborhood/container/python

or then again

#! /usr/receptacle/python

On the off chance that the penetrationway to the python parallel on your framework is unique, change that line, leaving the initial two characters (#!) flawless. Make certain this line is genuinely the principal line in your content, not simply the first non-clear line-it will spare you a ton of dissatisfaction.

Use chmod to set the record authorizations on your content to make it executable. On the off chance that the content is for only you, type chmod 0700 scriptfilename.py; on the off chance that you need to impart it to others in your gathering yet not let them alter it, utilize 0750 as the chmod esteem; on the off chance that you need to offer access to every other person, utilize the worth 0755. For assistance with the chmod order, type man chmod.

Perusing Command-Line Options and Arguments

Order line alternatives and contentions prove to

be useful when we need to advise our contents how to carry on or pass a few contentions (record names, catalog names, client names, and so on.) to them. All projects can peruse these alternatives and contentions in the event that they need, and your Python contents are the same.

Penetrationtesting which is additionally alluded to as pen testing or security testing is a training that includes assaulting data frameworks likewise an assailant would with the goal of recognizing vulnerabilities. The distinctive attributes of pen testing are no mischief is done on the frameworks and the assent of the proprietor of the framework is required. A powerlessness can be characterized as a security shortcoming that exists in a piece of a data framework that gives a section point to an assault. Vulnerabilities in a framework can emerge from bugs and blunders in structure and arrangement among others. The most widely recognized assault passage focuses are programs, social building, SQL infusion, streak, web 2.0 and ActiveX. In this article, we will examine Penetration Testing and Metasploit by the exhibit of windows establishment.

Because of various assault situations distinctive infiltration testing types are required. The three sorts of testing that can be utilized are discovery, white box and dark box testing. In discovery testing no data about the framework is given to the individual endeavor the testing. It is the obligation of the analyzer to assemble data about the framework. In white box testing total data about the objective framework is given. Such testing is extremely valuable for understanding the effect of an inward assault. In dim box testing the analyzer is given some data about the framework. Such a test gives a comprehension of the effect of an outside assault.

A Penetration Testing and Metasploit procedure can be separated into Four phases.

The principal stage is Planning the test. The target of the primary stage is distinguishing the degree and methodology of completing the test. The extent of the test is educated by right now rehearsed strategies and guidelines.

The second phase of testing is Discovery. There are three exercises that are done in this stage. The primary movement is gathering framework data and the information it holds. This action is alluded to as fingerprinting. The subsequent movement is examining and testing framework ports. The third action is distinguishing any vulnerabilities the framework may have.

The third phase of testing is Attack. This stage includes recognizing misuses for vulnerabilities. An endeavor is a PC program whose goal is to use a powerlessness so as to access a framework. In the wake of accessing a framework a payload is the product that empowers control of the traded off framework. The endeavor is utilized to convey the payload.

The fourth stage is Reporting. The goal of this stage is making an itemized report of distinguished vulnerabilities, their effect on business and arrangements.

In spite of the fact that there are numerous apparatuses to encourage penetrationtesting Metaspoilt is one of the generally utilized instruments. This instructional exercise will concentrate on showing utilization of Metaspoilt. Metasploit is offered as a free network version and a paid expert release which is accessible for a multi day preliminary. Metasploit is upheld on Windows, Ubuntu and Redhat working frameworks. The most recent forms of Chrome, Firefox and Internet Explorer are bolstered.

The Metasploit system is composed into modules. The primary kind of module is misuse. Endeavor modules are intended to exploit framework shortcomings. Models are cradle flood, application adventures and code infusion. Assistant modules perform activities that don't straightforwardly exploit shortcomings. For instance examining and administration forswearing. Post-abuse modules are gone for data assembling on objective frameworks. Payload modules pursue a shortcoming has been effectively abused. The payload gives the way to control an abused framework. With the payload you can open a meterpreter to compose DLL documents. NOP generator modules are for formation of irregular bytes to go around standard ID marks.

When I state "Entrance Testing device" the main thing that strikes a chord is the world's biggest Ruby venture, with more than 700,000 lines of code 'Metasploit' [Reference 1]. No big surprise it had turned into the accepted standard for infiltration testing and defenselessness improvement with more than one million exceptional downloads every year and the world's biggest, open database of value guaranteed misuses.

The Metasploit Framework is a program and sub-venture created by Metasploit LLC. It was at first made in 2003 in the Perl programming language, however was later totally re-written in the Ruby Programming Language. With the latest discharge (3.7.1) Metasploit has taken adventure testing and reproduction to a total new level which has built out its costly business partners by expanding the speed and lethality of code of endeavor in most brief conceivable time.

Entrance Testing with Metasploit Framework

Creator: Dinesh Shetty

See Also

File of all Anti-Spyware Tools

Nexpose + Metasploit = Shell

PDF - Vulnerabilities, Exploits and Malwares

DllHijackAuditor: Smart Tool to Audit Dll Hijack Vulnerability

SpyBHORemover - Quick Tool to Remove Spy BHO from the System.

Substance

Presentation

Working with Metasploit

Pen Testing utilizing Metasploit

Rundown

References

End

Presentation

When I state "Entrance Testing apparatus" the main thing that rings a bell is the world's biggest Ruby venture, with more than 700,000 lines of code 'Metasploit' [Reference 1]. No big surprise it had turned into the true standard for entrance testing and weakness improvement with more than one million exceptional downloads every year and the world's biggest, open database of value guaranteed misuses.

The Metasploit Framework is a program and sub-venture created by Metasploit LLC. It was at first made in 2003 in the Perl programming language, however was later totally re-written in the Ruby Programming Language. With the latest discharge (3.7.1) Metasploit has taken adventure testing and reenactment to a total new level which has built out its expensive business partners by expanding the speed and lethality of code of endeavor in most limited conceivable time.

Working with Metasploit

Metasploit is easy to utilize and is planned in view of convenience to help Penetration Testers.

Metasploit Framework pursues these regular advances while abusing an any objective framework

Select and design the endeavor to be focused on.

This is the code that will be focused toward a framework with the goal of exploiting an imperfection in the software. Validate whether the picked framework is defenseless to the picked adventure and arrange a payload that will be utilized. This payload speaks to the code that will be pursued on a framework an escape clause has been found in the framework and a section point is set.t.

Select and arrange the encoding construction to be utilized to ensure that the payload can sidestep Intrusion Detection Systems effortlessly.

Execute the endeavor.

I will take you through this demo in BackTrack 5 [Reference 2], so feel free to download that in the event that you don't as of now have it. The purpose behind utilizing BackTrack 5 is that it accompanies ideal arrangement for Metasploit and everything that Pen Testing individual ever need.

Metasploit structure has three workplaces, the msfconsole, the msfcli interface and the msfweb interface. Be that as it may, the essential and the most favored work region is the 'msfconsole'. It is a productive direction line interface that has its own order set and condition framework.

Tutorial

For this particular tutorial, a private network with a Kali machine and a Metasploitable machine was created.

This made things easier and safer since the private network range would ensure that scans remained on safe machines and prevents the vulnerable Metasploitable machine from being compromised by someone else.

How to Find Live Hosts on My Network?

In this example, both of the machines are on a private 192.168.10.0 /24 network. The Kali machine has an IP address of 192.168.10.101 and the Metasploitable machine to be scanned has an IP address of 192.168.10.102.

Let's say though that the IP address information was unavailable. A quick nmap scan can help to determine what is live on a particular network. This scan is known as a 'Simple List' scan hence the -sL arguments passed to the nmap command.

nmap -sL 192.168.10.0/24

Sadly, this initial scan didn't return any live hosts. Sometimes this is a factor of the way certain Operating Systems handle port scan network traffic.

Find and Ping All Live Hosts on My Network

There are some tricks that nmap has available to try to find these machines. This next trick will tell nmap to simply try to ping all the addresses in the 192.168.10.0/24 network.

nmap -sn 192.168.10.0/24

This time nmap returns some prospective hosts for scanning. In this command, the -sn disables nmap's default behavior of attempting to port scan a host and simply has nmap try to ping the host.

Find Open Ports on Hosts

Let's try letting nmap port scan these specific hosts and see what turns up.

nmap 192.168.10.1,100-102

Suppose that this particular host has some open network ports.

The open ports all indicate some sort of listening service on this particular machine. Recalling from earlier, the 192.168.10.102 IP address is assigned to the metasploitable vulnerable machine hence why there are so many open ports on this host.

Having many ports open on most machines is highly abnormal so it may be a wise idea to investigate this machine a little closer. Administrators could track down the physical machine on the network and look at the machine locally, but that wouldn't be much fun especially when nmap could do it for us much quicker!

Find Services Listening on Ports on Hosts

This next scan is a service scan and is often used to try to determine what service may be listening on a particular port on a machine.

Nmap will probe all of the open ports and attempt to banner grab information from the services running on each port.

nmap -sV 192.168.10.102

Notice this time nmap provided some suggestions on what nmap thought might be running on this particular port. Also nmap also tried to determine information about the operating system running on this machine as well as its hostname (with great success too!).

Looking through this output should raise quite a few concerns for a network administrator. Suppose that a line claims that VSftpd version 2.3.4 is running on this machine. That's a really old version of VSftpd.

Searching through ExploitDB, a serious vulnerability was found back in 2011 for this particular version (ExploitDB ID – 17491).

Find Anonymous FtP Logins on Hosts

Let's have nmap take a closer look at this particular port and see what can be determined.

nmap -sC 192.168.10.102 -p 21

With this command, nmap was instructed to run

its default script (-sC) on the FTP port (-p 21) on the host. While it may or may not be an issue, nmap did find out that anonymous FTP login is allowed on this particular server.

Check for Vulnerabilities on Hosts

This paired with the earlier knowledge about VSftd having an old vulnerability should raise some concern though. Let's see if nmap has any scripts that attempt to check for the VSftpd vulnerability.

locate .nse | grep ftp

Notice that nmap has a NSE script already built for the VSftpd backdoor problem. Let's try running this script against this host and see what happens but first it may be important to know how to use the script.

nmap --script-help=ftp-vsftd-backdoor.nse

Reading through its description, it is clear that this script can be used to attempt to see if this particular machine is vulnerable to ExploitDB issue identified earlier.

Let's run the script and see what happens.

nmap --script=ftp-vsftpd-backdoor.nse 192.168.10.102 -p 21

If Nmap's script returns some dangerous news, the machine is likely a good candidate for a serious investigation. This doesn't mean that the machine is compromised and being used for terrible things but it should bring some concerns to the network/security teams.

Nmap has the ability to be extremely selective and extremely quite. Most of what has been done so far has attempted to keep nmap's network traffic moderately quiet however scanning a personally owned network in this fashion can be extremely time consuming.

Nmap has the ability to do a much more aggressive scan that will often yield much of the same information but in one command instead of several. Let's take a look at the output of an aggressive scan (Do note – an aggressive scan can set off intrusion detection/prevention systems!).

nmap -A 192.168.10.102

Notice this time, with one command, nmap returns a lot of the information it returned earlier about the open ports, services, and configurations running on this particular machine. Much of this information can be used to help determine how to protect this machine as well as to evaluate what software may be on a network.

This was just a short, short list of the many useful things that nmap can be used to find on a host or network segment. It is strongly urged that individuals continue to experiment with nmap in a controlled manner on a network that is owned by the individual (do not practice by scanning other entities!).